Managing Your Money
Surviving Any Economy

Managing Your Money

Surviving Any Economy

Bonnie Raney O'Brien

iUniverse, Inc.

New York   Bloomington

Managing Your Money
Surviving Any Economy

iUniverse books may be ordered through booksellers or by contacting:

iUniverse
1663 Liberty Drive
Bloomington, IN 47403
www.iuniverse.com
1-800-Authors (1-800-288-4677)

ISBN: 978-1-4401-2090-9 (pbk)
ISBN: 978-1-4401-2091-6 (ebk)

Printed in the United States of America

iUniverse rev. date: 2/9/2009

To my son, Michael – always my inspiration – and to Karin, my friend and editor.

Contents

Introduction

During the last 35 years, there have been five recessions; the last few have been relatively mild ones. If you're 43 years old or younger, you haven't previously experienced a truly tough economy.

When consumers lose confidence in the economy, it causes a downward spiral. The depression of the 1930s was overturned by spending programs administered by the government. Our grandparents learned how to save money instead of spend it.

Following the depression and after World War II, our parents' generation developed a post-war sense of living for the moment, which was further exacerbated by the Cold War and the threat of nuclear destruction. "Time payments" were promoted as the ex-GI's means to having it all, and new technology was producing "all–affordable" housing, automobiles, automatic washers and dryers, televisions, private-line telephones, and much more. The concept of living on credit was born.

Recent recessions have been spawned by out-of-control borrowing. People have maxed out their credit limits by living beyond their means, spending way more than their earnings and treating plastic cards as free passes. The borrowing spree suddenly results in a "black hole" when the economy starts its downward trend again.

We must not panic, however. Panic is what turns a recession into a depression. The economy is cyclical, and if you take action during the downturn, you'll survive to enjoy the upswing. If you have the money, reassess your investments and take advantage of the opportunities, such as real estate bargains and purchasing equities unloaded by others, presented by an economic downturn.

If you have debt and can't afford to tear up your credit cards, call your lenders to negotiate better interest rates. Most creditors expect this and will work with you. The worst that can happen is that they'll say no.

First, you need a budget and an emergency fund. People who budget and plan have money. If you're in debt, you need to figure out where you spent it and how to start paying it back.

A recession is the economy's reminder to have a savings plan. People with savings, diversified investments and no debt can survive any economy, even if they lose their jobs. It all goes back to living within your means and not spending more than you earn.

Develop a network of like-thinking friends who will work together to develop a flexible strategy to survive.

A little effort can save you thousands of dollars a year!

Attitudes/Behavior

In this day and age, it's all about "disposable". Unfortunately, that has become society's mind-set. We need to start thinking "indisposable".

Maturity is taking responsibility for ourselves and our actions, acknowledging our problems and the role we played in them, and seeking solutions. When it comes to money, many of us choose to forget that responsibility, blaming others (parents, children, governments, lenders) for the fixes we're in. Housing, food, clothing, transportation and how we spend our time are all personal choices that have a great impact on our financial situation.

It may seem that everyone else seems to be spending freely while we're counting pennies. We may resent not being able to just once buy something we want without worrying about the consequences. Trying to "keep up with the Joneses" may be what got us into financial trouble in the first place. The Joneses may not be as well off as they seem and may also be struggling with debt; this can make keeping up with them a little less attractive. The average family has $8,000 in credit card debt; as soon as you only owe $7,999, you're better than average.

We need to pay even closer attention to expenses when focusing on surviving economic down trends. Retailers and entertainment media, including theaters, casinos, and liquor stores, historically show increased sales during recessions as people lean toward escapism during tough economic times. This is when people tend toward daydreaming, gambling, drinking and spending, mistakenly hoping these actions will solve their problems. We can't expect lottery tickets, stock market analysts or other outside forces to solve our financial problems. We need to stop fantasizing and take charge of our own finances now!

A healthier way to temporarily escape our situation is to volunteer for a cause or charity; this can be much more rewarding and it's free. If you previously donated cash, you might consider replacing the cash donation with material goods or an in-kind contribution of your time. These may also be tax deductible.

We need to change the way we think about and behave with money; "nothing changes if nothing changes" – we can't continue to do the same things we've done in the past and expect different results.

We can't manage our money if we don't know how much we have coming in and how much is going out. Write down your five biggest money problems: Credit card debt? Big mortgage payment? Lack of cash? Lack of savings?

Identify your role in creating those problems: What choices did you make that put you in this position? Even if you're not entirely to blame (life events impact us all), what decisions or actions did you make that made matters worse? Some examples are:

Spent more than I made

Lack an emergency fund

Failed to carefully review the terms of a loan

Neglected to have a plan

Procrastinated on dealing with an issue until it became a bigger problem

Brainstorm some solutions. Try to think of every possible solution you can, no matter how strange or unusual some of them may seem. If you get stumped, look online for suggestions or experiences of others who have faced and overcome similar situations.

Make a plan -- and follow through. Pick some solutions and act on them. For example, if you're behind on your mortgage payments, talk to a housing counselor; if you lack a budget, create one; if you're mired in credit card debt, contact a legitimate credit counseling agency, a bankruptcy attorney, or both.

Taking responsibility, taking action, and taking control of your finances empowers you and ultimately leads to financial freedom and its resultant peace of mind. Whether you're paying off debt, saving more or just living within your means, you're working at avoiding the fear and stress of people who are not in control of their finances. Remembering this can help you stick to your plan and get you to your goal that much quicker.

Even the most diligent planning can't always ward off life events and setbacks.

- *Plan for contingencies.* Many budgets fail because they are not realistic and/or flexible enough. When budgeting, be conservative with income and liberal with expenses. One of the most important steps to take is to keep a wide margin, by saving more and living on less, between how much you have and how much you're likely to need. This is tough when things are tight, so build the best cushion you can, saving at least only $10 or $20 a week. You might also consider a major life change, such as reducing your rent by moving to a less expensive home or neighborhood.

- *Discriminate unexpected expenses.* Be sure to distinguish between the surprise expenses you need to spend money on and those you could avoid. Think about how easy it is to spend an extra $10 or $20 a day on what may seem like bona fide "unexpected expenses", such as a sandwich because you're working late (a possible solution would be to keep a supply of nutritious snacks on hand at work, such as protein bars). By avoiding frivolous expenses, you can save money for those unexpected costs that are truly unavoidable.

- *Save more.* Save 10% of your gross income. If you can't afford 10% right away, start by saving 5%. Then, once saving becomes second nature to you and as soon as you can, increase it to 10%. If you're just rebuilding your finances, even saving $10 to $20 per paycheck is a positive beginning. As your income increases, increase your percentage of savings. Also, be sure to save a predetermined dollar amount per month in your separate emergency fund account, and $10 or $20 a week in a separate vacation fund account, if possible**. Make it a habit to pay your savings accounts first, before any expenses.**

- *Stop bad spending habits.* Stay organized and aware of all expenses. Review your budget and bank account balances often and regularly, at least 1-2 times per week, to avoid being blindsided by sudden expenses.

- *Conserve cash.* The biggest reason unexpected expenses can take such a toll is the general lack of cash, usually the result of careless spending. Start with building one small habit by doing the same thing every day or week, ideally at the same time each day or week. For example, take out $20 a week in cash and don't spend it (hide it away somewhere so that it's out of sight and out of mind). The next week do the same thing. This way you create a positive weekly non-spending habit. You can then add the cash to your savings, or you'll have some cash available for legitimate unexpected expenses. Like every good habit, this takes practice.

Banking

- *Look for banks with no checking account fees.*
- *Consider an interest-bearing checking account.*
- *Avoid ATM fees.* Make as few withdrawals as possible at ATM machines that will incur fees; withdraw at your own bank's ATM if no fee is charged, or withdraw extra cash at a supermarket or other store when making a purchase.
- *Shop for the best interest on savings accounts.*
- *Consider opening your savings accounts at a bank other than your checking account bank.* This makes your savings less accessible.
- *Keep tabs on your balance.* Overdraft and bounced check fees add up fast. If you use a debit card vs. your checkbook, jot down all your debit transactions on your checkbook register, or keep track electronically, to make sure you know how much money is in your bank account at all times.
- *Evaluate your spending.* If you need help with this, there are some free online programs, such as wesabe.com and mint.com. You enter your accounts on one convenient site. The program can also help you pinpoint areas for improvement, and protects your passwords, identity and data.

Spending

Following are some economic and financial concepts:

1. Our resources, whether oil, time, or cash, have limits; there's only so much available to spend. People who ignore this run out of a paycheck before they run out of a month, or increase their spending by relying on credit cards, home equity loans and other borrowing. Refusal to make hard choices and manage money responsibly results in even fewer future choices. Money spent on material items and on interest can't be invested in other goals, like retirement and savings. This leads to devastating financial consequences for us in our later years.

2. For every money decision/choice, there's an opportunity cost. Opportunity cost is defined as what we give up to get something else. For example, if we go to college, we give up the income we could have earned by working full-time during those years plus whatever we could have purchased with the money used for school. But, going to college and training for a career that has little demand could result in making no more than a high school graduate and possibly being saddled with large student loan debt we can never repay. We may then regret the money spent on school and the lost income from not working. Understanding that our choices have opportunity costs, and what those costs are, will help us make better financial decisions.

3. For the most part, prices are set by supply and demand. If demand for something shoots up and the available supply of that something doesn't change, prices will increase. If demand drops or the supply increases, prices typically fall. For example, a new toy is marketed just before the holidays and suddenly everyone wants one (witness the Cabbage Patch Kid or Tickle Me Elmo phenom). The

toy stores stock up on the toy and increase the price. The manufacturer then wants a piece of the action and starts making more and more of this toy.

Suddenly you can find one in every store. The toy stores can no longer command a premium for having a special item, due to the increase in supply. Once this toy is no longer considered to be so special, demand for it decreases. Retailers then cut the price still further to get rid of their unwanted supplies. Supply and demand have a lot to do with our incomes as well. If we have rare skills that are in high demand by employers, we can negotiate higher pay. Conversely, if a lot of people can do what we do or the employer demand for what we do is limited, our incomes will be lower.

4. "Sunk costs" are expenses that have already been incurred and can't be recovered. "Sunk cost fallacy" is the belief that a further investment of time, money or effort will somehow resurrect the value that's already disappeared; in other words, "throwing good money after bad". A classic example is the investor whose stock has plunged because the prospects of the company have worsened. The investor wouldn't buy the same stock today, but continues to hang on to the shares rather than sell them and take the loss. The investor may offer the excuse that he or she wants to at least break even before selling; however, the stock market doesn't care whether the investor gets the money back or not, and all the wishing in the world won't bring the stock price back up. By hanging on to the shares, the investor is giving up the opportunity to invest in something else at a profit -- an opportunity cost.

5. Every human endeavor, including investment of money, carries some risk. What differs is the amount and type of risk and how you're compensated for taking it. For example, if you invest all your money in a single stock,

like Enron, you could be wiped out. That's called market risk. You need to take some market risk if you want to grow your wealth and beat inflation over time. However, you also need to be cautious of any "guarantees" of a high investment return.

6. The dollar you get today is worth more than a dollar you're promised for sometime in the future. First, the dollar you get today is real, whereas the dollar you're promised for the future will most certainly be worth less due to inflation. You may not even get it due to unforeseen circumstances, such as an unfulfilled promise, death, or sudden unemployment. Second, the dollar you get today can be invested to create more dollars in the future. With this concept in mind, you can see why lenders charge interest for loaning money and why the interest rate depends on your creditworthiness. Lenders want to be compensated for the erosion in their dollars due to inflation, and for the risk of lending money to you. The higher the perceived rate of future inflation and the more doubt lenders have in your ability to repay them, the more interest they'll charge to compensate for the risk.

7. The concept of compounded interest is best illustrated by example. Let's say I give you a penny today, and promise to double the amount every day for a full month:

Day 1	$	0.01
Day 2	$	0.02
Day 3	$	0.04
Day 4	$	0.08
Day 5	$	0.16
Day 6	$	0.32
Day 7	$	0.64
Day 8	$	1.28
Day 9	$	2.56
Day 10	$	5.12
Day 11	$	10.24
Day 12	$	20.48
Day 13	$	40.96
Day 14	$	81.92
Day 15	$	163.84
Day 16	$	327.68
Day 17	$	655.36
Day 18	$	1,310.72
Day 19	$	2,621.44
Day 20	$	5,242.88
Day 21	$	10,485.76
Day 22	$	20,971.52
Day 23	$	41,943.04
Day 24	$	83,886.08
Day 25	$	167,772.16
Day 26	$	335,544.32
Day 27	$	671,088.64
Day 28	$	1,342,177.28
Day 29	$	2,684,354.56
Day 30	$	5,368,709.12
Day 31	$	10,737,418.24

Each day, the "interest" I paid you the previous day earns more interest. At the beginning, the amounts are nominal, but by the end we're talking about well over $10 million! Of course, no one's going to double your money every day. But this example does show how people who save relatively small amounts over the years can build substantially large nest eggs. After a few decades, their actual contributions represent only a small part of their growing wealth; it's mostly their returns that are earning returns.

However, this also shows how debts can quickly balloon out of control. If you're paying interest and not paying off the balance in full every month, the unpaid amount will incur additional interest charges, increasing the total amount that you owe. This is why so many people who incur credit card debt ultimately find themselves in trouble as the amounts they owe explode past their ability to pay.

Every dollar you don't spend is a dollar you've earned and saved. Before making any purchase, always ask yourself "Do I really need this?" When tempted to make a purchase, physically walk away from the item for 10 minutes; then see if the urge to purchase is still as strong.

If you determine a true need, then ask "How can I get it free, or almost free?" Explore thrift shops, rummage sales, flea markets, and online sites like Craigslist.org. Watch for coupons and sales. You can also buy Christmas and birthday gifts from the same vendors. No one need know that the hardback bestseller under the tree cost you only 50 cents.

Track your spending. If you don't know where your money goes, you need to find out. You can:

- Carry a notebook and pen to write down every expenditure, or use a paper calendar to track not only the bills that are due on certain dates but the amounts you spend each day. Go through your checkbook and credit card statements. Add up the amounts, and you'll have a good idea about your spending habits.
- Try an online tracker like Wesabe**,** Geezeo**,** Mint or use a spreadsheet program like Microsoft Excel to organize your spending into different categories

- Use personal finance software such as Money or Quicken to download your bank and credit card transactions into your computer to help manage them.

Budget and live within your means. Those who are chronically short of cash often overspend on the large things, especially their home and car.

- Develop a six-month plan to reduce any expenses or increase any income. The plan should be implemented immediately so you can realize the results at the end of the six months. Select one or two realistic expenses to start with. Also, income may be increased by working part-time during that six-month period.
- Spend only on essentials.
- Research every purchase; learn how to do lots of things yourself (car repair, hair cutting, sewing, cooking, home maintenance, etc.)
- Stop buying things you can't afford.
- Review all of your recurring expenses, such as car insurance, phone and internet bills, and utilities. Compare services and get new quotes; some companies offer a discount if you pay upfront, which can help you save some money and reduce your monthly expenses.
- Don't fall victim to vices (drinking, gambling, drugging); wasting money won't help you survive an economy.

Needs vs. Wants
Hedonic treadmill

Economists have coined the term "hedonic treadmill". It works like this:

1. You really want something (big screen TV, dining room set, iPod, car, house).
2. After much craving, you buy the item.

3. You're thrilled for a short while.

4. The thrill fades.

5. You start to feel empty and crave that emotional high, a sense of accomplishment or of "being good enough."

6. You decide that what you REALLY want is something else (refrigerator, designer suit, jewelry, vacation, deck).

7. The whole thing starts all over again.

One of the biggest factors that keep people on the hedonic treadmill is the tendency to compare their lot with others' – "keeping up with the Joneses" (*see Attitudes/Behavior*) -- keeping up with the material acquisitions of those around us.

If, however, we decide to step off the treadmill for financial and emotional sanity, we may still face social pressure from family or friends who are on this treadmill themselves or who may have different financial priorities or philosophies.

Whether we don't have money because we're trying to get out of debt, got laid off or just had a new child, it's easy to be influenced by friends and family who spend freely. Feeling like the "odd man out" can be painful, and we need ways to cope:

- *Appearances can be deceiving.* Friends may be subsidized by parents or wealthier siblings, or may be relying on credit cards and loans. We can get trapped in the illusion of how our lives ought to be.

- *You're not the center of attention.* When we feel different in any way it feels as though others are focusing on us. Most people are concerned with and wrapped up in their own lives; they aren't paying that much attention to ours.

- *Be honest.* Admit, 'I can't afford to do this, but I do want to spend time with you." Suggest a dinner at home, a trip to a museum, or a free concert. Friends would rather you care about them more than about what it is you're doing together.

- *Have the courage of your convictions.*
- *Move past your fears.* When we change our financial habits and practices, we may be afraid that friends and family will be insulted or think we're cheap.

When we can't distinguish between real needs and mere wants, we're constantly talking ourselves into spending too much. An example is: We **need** food. We **want** prime rib.

It's more the little things, such as eating out, that we "splurge" on, as opposed to big-ticket items that often prevent us from reaching financial goals. Consumers have also expanded the list of things they deem to be necessities; for instance, a microwave oven, an air conditioned car, a home computer and a cell phone.

However, the majority also believe they should be saving more. A recent survey[1] found that almost one quarter of Americans feel that their most important financial goal is just keeping up with bills. Another quarter said their biggest undertaking is paying down debt. Meanwhile, saving for retirement, putting kids through college, and purchasing a home ranked further down the list.

From the Pew survey on Americans' spending and saving habits:

Which kind of expense do you splurge on the most?

Expense	Percentage
Food and dining out	25
Entertainment & recreation	17
Shopping & personal items	15
Home & housing	7
Children & schooling	7
Bills & utilities	4
Cars	3
Medical	1
Other	4
Nothing	14
Don't know	6

Note: Responses total more than 100% because respondents could offer more than one answer.

Source: Pew Research Center

What do we actually *need*?

1. *A roof over our heads.* We don't necessarily need a house as nice as the one we live in; in many cases, we could make do with something smaller or older. Therefore, probably half of our mortgage payment is a need and half of it is a want. The same is true of homeowners insurance; many people's homes are over insured.

2. *Food and water.* Most of our food bill should consist of staples and basic needs. If you pay for your water, obviously that bill is also a need.

3. *Clothing.* "Wear it out or do without." Start with a basic quality wardrobe and buy to mix and match; this can multiply your wardrobe as much as tenfold. Quality (not necessarily inordinately expensive) clothing will last

longer. *(See Clothing & Personal Care)*

4. *Basic hygiene and health.* This spending is largely needs-based; however, many people do spend excessive amounts on hygiene products. Don't be misled by marketing "hype"; for example, how many "nutrients" can there be in one shampoo?

5. *Electricity.* Even though this is a basic need, we still have some control over the expense. Turning off lights when leaving a room is one way. For other tips, *see Utilities*.

6. *Heat in the winter or air conditioning in warmer climates.* These are certainly needs in the more extreme climates. As with the other needs, there are ways to control these expenses; see *Utilities* for some suggestions.

7. *A stream of income to pay for the needs.* In our current society and economy, rarely can a family survive without both members of a couple earning income.

8. *Transportation.* Regardless of the type of transportation (car, bus, train), unless you live within walking distance of work and shopping, this is a necessary expense. For some help with managing this expense, see the *Transportation* section of this book.

Everything else is a *want*.

When we look at the few things in our life that are actually needs, we can see how many things we buy simply because we want them and how much fat we can really cut.

For instance, if you already pay for a cell phone, high-speed Internet and have a computer with a microphone and speakers, you might consider Skype. This would replace a land line phone. Also, consider getting a prepaid cell phone, which would reduce the cell phone expense as well.

The objective is to realize how much of your monthly spending goes toward wants. Wanting things is normal and fine as long as you're not abandoning sound financial responsibility just to maintain the things you want.

Eliminating some wants and focusing more on the most important things leads to cuts in spending and big changes in spending choices. This results in more cash and/or savings.

(***Try this:*** Divide all your spending into needs and wants. For every dollar you spend on a want, put a dollar into savings for the future.)

The benefits of changing spending habits are more time to give to others and more money to save. We gain a sense of control and optimism about our financial future. We learn what we can live without and how we really want to spend our money. All of this results in a peace of mind that previously eluded us.

Shopping

- *Avoid stores.* Stay out of stores unless you have a list (mental or otherwise) of specific things you need to buy. Shopping out of boredom leads to impulse buying and can quickly destroy a budget.
- *Buy what you need when it goes on sale, if you can wait.*
- *When you need to buy something, consider buying higher-quality items* at stores that stand behind what they sell. That way, if anything wears out or quits working before its time, you can return or exchange it. Also when buying (in-store or online), diligently look for and carefully review warrantees and return policies. You can save money by buying things of higher quality that last longer than by buying cheaper items that you have to throw away and replace again or frequently.

- *Carefully compare the cost of buying items online* -- including shipping and handling charges, cost of gas and your time -- with the cost of in-store buying. Online shipping/handling charges can add up quickly and result in a sizeable amount of wasted money; however, there are times when it is more cost-effective than shopping in-store.

- *Avoid buying any unnecessary big-ticket items* (stoves, refrigerators, a new car).

- *Reduce the number and cost of gifts*, especially at Christmastime; you can give yourself and your services as gifts -- do your mate's chores for a day or weekend, give a person a massage yourself, make a special meal for someone, or babysit for someone. To reduce the cost of purchased gifts, shop at church bazaars, rummage sales, thrift shops, dollar stores, and online sites, such as Amazon.com and Craigslist.org.

- *Consider cutting back on subscriptions,* such as newspapers, to the bare minimum. If you only get a paper once a week, choose the Sunday paper. This edition usually includes coupons and weekly sales flyers from local grocery stores. Toss any other sales flyers; they may tempt you to buy other things you don't need.

- *Find new uses for old things;* for example, when changing or adding oil to your car, recirculate an old plastic milk jug by cutting away the bottom half and using the remaining top as a funnel to reduce spillage. This saves a trip to the auto store to buy a funnel, saves money, and helps to keep our planet greener!

Many of us waste our hard-earned money every day by buying new. We could do our pocketbooks, and the environment, a favor by opting for second-hand.

Obviously, some things, such as undergarments, are best purchased new. But many other items depreciate quickly while still having plenty of useful life. Following are 9 items that are surefire second-hand bargains:

1. *Books* - Most books don't get read more than once and can easily be found at steep discounts -- if not absolutely free. If you can't find a particular book at your local library, they may allow you to reserve titles for delivery to your nearest branch for pick-up. Used book stores are plentiful, both in your area and online. Also, don't forget yard sales.

2. *DVDs and CDs* - Like books, most DVDs aren't viewed more than once or twice. Some online retailers, like MSN Shopping and Amazon.com, now sell used versions of many of the DVD movies they sell new. You can find similar online deals for CDs. Movie rental chains like Blockbuster, used record stores, and yard sales also offer used items.

3. *Children's toys* - Shop consignment shops and yard sales for bargains. This is particularly advantageous at holiday time, when overspending runs rampant. Parents know how susceptible children are to TV and print retailer advertising during this season. However, we also know that what a child thinks he wants today is already old hat and replaced by a new I-want-that tomorrow! If you *must*, buy one popular toy new (as long as it's reasonably priced) and others second-hand. You can also mix new and second-hand clothing items for gifts.

4. *Jewelry* - 100% markups on most gems can result in a quick 2/3 depreciation; this means that you'll be lucky to get 1/3 of what you paid at a retail store if you ever need to sell. Find a pawn shop that's been in business for awhile, get to know the owner and ask him or her for recommendations. When buying second-hand jewelry,

whenever possible, get the piece appraised at a reputable jeweler first or at least get an assurance that if it is not appraised for its stated value, you can return it. If you want something new (for yourself or for a gift), consider buying used stones and getting them reset. A most valued gift is a family "heirloom" gem in an updated setting.

5. *Sports equipment* - So much fitness equipment is bought with good intentions and left to collect dust. Buy someone else's good intention for some substantial savings. Shop yard sales, local newspaper ads, resale stores, and online.

6. *Cars* - The average new car loses 12+% of its value in the first year; that's $2,440 on a $20,000 car, or more than $200 a month. Some cars depreciate even faster. Buying a used car means that not only will you be able to save money (or buy more car), but you'll pay less for insurance. Companies like CarFax allow you to trace a car's history. Many late-model used cars are still under warranty, and a trusted mechanic can examine your potential purchase for any problems. Take a look at the Used Car Research section of MSN Autos for a lot of great information. *Also, see Transportation.*

7. *Software and console games* - You can pay half or less what the software costs new by buying used games like those for Xbox 360 and Sony PlayStation 3.30 a year after release. Let someone else be the early adopter and "debugger" of new software. You'll also find more reviews and information on software that's been out a year or more.

    Caution: Some software restricts the number of computers on which it can be installed, which can make it difficult (but not impossible) to transfer the product license to a new owner.

8. *Office furniture* - Good-quality office desks, filing

cabinets and credenzas are relatively easy to find.

Caution: Whenever possible, try out at least any chair you may consider buying to make sure it's a good fit.

- *Hand tools* - If you don't use a particular tool frequently, you may be able to rent it or borrow from a friend or neighbor rather than buying it new. Some neighborhoods even run tool-sharing cooperatives. If you do intend to buy, well-made hand tools, such as hammers, wrenches, shovels, hoes, etc., can last decades with proper maintenance and can be easy to find at yard sales. Power tools can have a relatively limited life span, so you may want to buy those new if you'll use them often.

Timing is everything! Try timing your purchases to coincide with manufacturer discounts, clearance sales and off-season discounts. Following are some best times of the year to shop:

- *Airline tickets* - **S**ome carriers file their lowest fares as a 21-day advance purchase; the next window is at 14 days. Getting a good ticket price depends on where you're flying to and from and the number of available seats. Airlines typically file updates to their fares three times a day: 10 a.m., 12:30 p.m. and 8 p.m. weekdays, and one 5:00 p.m. filing on Saturday and Sunday (all times are ET). Most of the lowest fares are filed Tuesdays, Wednesdays and sometimes Saturdays, depending on the carrier and the market.[2]

- *Air conditioners*- Best time to buy: *Winter* Air conditioners' peak usage is May through September. As the demand increases and the stock is depleted, the price rises accordingly. Conversely, as cooler weather sets in and most people aren't interested in buying air conditioners, the demand for them decreases and prices drop.[3]

- **Big appliances** - Best time to buy: **September and October** New models of major appliances, such as ranges and washing machines, hit showroom floors in September and October, resulting in last year's models going on sale to make room. [3]

- **Bicycles and outdoor gear** - Best time to buy: **January** Stores start replacing fall and winter gear with spring and summer models in February. Therefore, post-holiday sales are your best bet for most outdoor gear, including shoes, bikes, hiking gear, etc.[4]

- **Computers** - Best time to buy: **July and August** You can save some money by buying slightly older technology vs. brand new. A good rule of thumb is to buy in the middle of the summer during back-to-school sales or in the winter during post-holiday sales.[5]

- **Cookware** - Best times to buy: **April and May, October and November** The two big seasons for cookware promotions are in the spring, coinciding with the graduation and wedding season, and in the fall, during pre-holiday promotions.[6]

- **Furniture** - Best times to buy: **January and July** In January, after the holidays, stores have clearance sales to make room for new inventory coming in February. In July, the same thing happens with fall inventory; for instance, it may be the same wooden frame for sofas with different upholstery in new colors for fall.[7]

- **Gas grills** - Best time to buy: **Winter** Timing for the best deal on barbecue grills is the same as shopping for air conditioners; wait until the cooler weather when the demand is low.[3]

- **Linens and bedding** - Best time to buy: **January** Bargains can be found on the previous season's styles for spring, summer, fall and winter; but traditionally, the biggest bargain is during January white sales.[8]

- ***Real estate*** - Best time to buy: ***Spring*** The real estate buying and selling season starts in March and goes through the summer. In the spring inventory and competition are highest, and there are more homes to choose from. Homes and landscaping look their best during this season. However, bargain hunters may prefer to do some negotiating in the fall and winter.[9]

- ***TVs*** - Best time to buy: ***Winter holiday sales and January*** New TV models arrive in stores in August and September, dropping in price a few months later and knocking down the price on older models.

- ***Vacuum cleaners*** - Best time to buy: ***April and May*** Most new vacuum models come out in June. The prices on the older models start decreasing as winter comes to a close, just in time for spring.[3]

- ***Wedding*** - Best time to buy: ***Winter*** Getting married during the off-season can net big savings. Demands for wedding services slow during the cold months (or in a tropical climate, the hot months).

1 GkF Roper Consulting
2 Farecompare.com
3 Home Appliance Magazine
4 Outside magazine
5 CNET
6 Cookware Manufacturers Association
7 American Home Furnishing Alliance
8 Cuddletown
9 National Association of Realtors

Budgeting

A budget shows us where our money goes and helps us to reach our financial goals, whether it's a new home, a comfortable retirement or just making it to the next paycheck. We simply can't spend more than we make. We need to constantly evaluate our spending and update our budget, using a constructive approach. If we **_don't_** get into the habit of budgeting, we may also face possible charges, such as:

Paying rent or mortgage late	$15 - $25 late fee
Paying utilities late	Percentage late fee (1%)
Paying a credit card late	$25 late fee
Insufficient funds	$25 - $30

(Actual fees may vary.)

Paying bills late will not only cost you but will also damage your credit record. This can hurt your ability to make future purchases on credit, such as buying a house or a car.

Building a Budget

Budgeting consists of four main steps:

Research   **Build**   **Monitor**   **Evaluate**

The first step is determining where your money goes. Once you know where you're spending your money, it's easier to find places to trim expenses so you can redirect the money into debt repayment or savings. This is especially true if you're broke or always struggling to make ends meet. You need to track your expenses, every single penny, either on paper or electronically for at least 2 weeks, preferably for a month, so you can make intelligent decisions about where and how to trim. You can use a small memo book that fits in your pocket or purse to track your daily spending. Below is an example of one page:

Monday		
Item	**Amount**	**Type**
Parking	4.25	cs
Coffee	1.50	cs
New book	7.48	cs
Fast food	6.25	cs
Groceries	23.00	dc
Dry Cleaning	8.50	ck
Gas	20.00	cr
ATM fee	1.75	dc
Total Day	**$72.73**	

Payment type:

cs = cash

ck = check

dc = debit card

cr = credit card

Source: PNC Bank

When you've completed tracking your spending for the two weeks, or month, you can see your spending habits and detect any trends or patterns. You can also determine which are necessary expenditures and which aren't. Consolidate your daily expenses into weekly, biweekly, or monthly totals – depending on your paycheck frequency. The totals of your necessary expenses will be included in your budget.

Then,

1.   Draw up a ***realistic*** budget. Try to plan for some savings, even if it's only $25 or $50/month to start. "Pay yourself first" (tough to do when bills are due, but try to stick to it; otherwise, saving won't happen). You'll find a way to pay the bills, but you won't find a way to save.

Some common budget categories include housing (rent or mortgage, homeowner dues), recurring bills (cable, utilities, insurance and credit card payments), food and entertainment. You might also have expenses for other items, such as pet care or travel. If your hobby is your passion, make it a category.

2. Account for big expenses that occur once or twice a year, such as car insurance. Total up these kinds of expenses, including non-escrowed real estate taxes, homeowners or tenants insurance, etc. for the year, then divide by 12. Put that monthly amount aside in a separate savings account until the bills are due.

3. Consider making your vehicle its own category; include payments, maintenance & repairs, and car insurance (see above regarding totaling some expenses for the year, then dividing by 12).

You may want to meet with an affordable reputable financial adviser (one you have to pay, not a freebie) to set your goals, make a plan/budget, and have a resource for support and help.

Below is a sample budget:

Paycheck Budget

(paid every two weeks)

Item	Amt.	Due	5-Aug	19-Aug	2-Sep	16-Sep	30-Sep
Paydates (with Net Income shown in the square below)							
Every pay items:			$ 1,047	$ 1,047	$ 1,047	$ 1,047	$ 1,047
Grocery store	$ 80	every					
Eating out	$ 20	every					
Transportation	$ 50	every					
401K Retirement	$ 80	every					
Long-term Savings	$ 25	every					
Church ($5/wk)	$ 10	every					
Entertainment	$ 30	every					
Babysitting	$ 40	every					
Monthly items:							
Rent/mortgage	$ 600	1st					
Electric	$ 100	1st					
Heat	$ 100	1st					
Phone	$ 30	15th					
Car payment	$ 250	15th					
Credit card 1	$ 50	15th					
Credit card 2	$ 50	20th					
Cable TV	$ 54	15th					
Finance fees	$ 6	20th					
Other regular items:							
Hair	$ 15	3wks					
Car insurance	$ 200	6 mos					
Tenants insurance	$ 120	6 mos					
Occasional items:							
Clothes	$ 30	per mo					
Furnishings	$ 10	per mo					
Gifts	$ 300	per yr					
Vacation	?	per yr					
Repairs	as needed						
Total Expenses							
Difference (Income-Expenses)							
Short-term Savings (cumulative)							

Once you've budgeted your monthly expenses, go through your pay stubs and calculate your average monthly income; include any regular bonuses, spousal support, etc. Try not to include non-regular income, such as commissions or dividends. Hopefully you don't need to rely on this type of inconsistent income to live within your means. When you receive this income, you can immediately add it to your savings, treating it as if it doesn't even exist. This can add up to substantial dollars quickly.

When you know how much you earn and how much you actually spend, decide where and how much you ***need*** or want to spend. This is your monthly budget. Adjust as necessary until your monthly expenses equal no more than your monthly income. If necessary, you may need to work overtime or take a second job, at least for a while.

Some things to keep in mind:

- Figure out which of your expenses are wants and which are needs. Actual needs are fairly limited (*see Needs vs. Wants*), but even the way we fulfill those needs involves some choice.

- Ideally, essential spending should be covered by the first 60% of your income. The rest includes retirement, emergencies, debt repayment, and fun money.

- Prioritize. Fund your retirement first, **no matter what**. Put enough in your 401(k) to get the employer match. Then start addressing your debts.

- Don't forget an emergency fund. This will go a long way toward keeping you out of debt when unexpected expenses arise. If you don't currently have an emergency savings fund, use your income-tax refund or set up a regular electronic transfer from checking to savings (*see emergency fund*).

Paycheck Budget

(paid every two weeks)

Paydates (with Net Income shown in the square below)							
Item	Amt.	Due	5-Aug	19-Aug	2-Sep	16-Sep	30-Sep
Every pay items:			$ 1,047	$ 1,047	$ 1,047	$ 1,047	$ 1,047
Grocery store	$ 80	every	80	80	80	80	80
Eating out	$ 20	every	20	50	20	20	20
Transportation	$ 50	every	50	50	50	50	50
401K Retirement	$ 80	every	80	80	80	80	80
Long-term Savings	$ 25	every	25	25	25	25	25
Church ($5/wk)	$ 10	every	10	10	10	10	10
Entertainment	$ 30	every	30	**100**	30	30	30
Babysitting	$ 40	every	40	**50**	40	40	40
Monthly items:							
Rent/mortgage	$ 600	1st		600			600
Electric	$ 100	1st		100			100
Heat	$ 100	1st		100			100
Phone	$ 30	15th	30		30		
Car payment	$ 250	15th	250		250		
Credit card 1	$ 50	15th	50		50		
Credit card 2	$ 50	20th		50		50	
Cable TV	$ 54	15th	54		54		
Finance fees	$ 6	20th		6		6	
Other regular items:							
Hair	$ 15	3wks		15	15		15
Car insurance	$ 200	6 mos				200	
Tenants insurance	$ 120	6 mos				120	
Occasional items:							
Clothes	$ 30	per mo	30		30		
Furnishings	$ 10	per mo		10		10	
Gifts	$ 300	per yr		24		24	
Vacation	?	per yr					
Repairs	as needed						
Total Expenses			749	1350	764	745	1150
Difference (Income-Expenses)			298	-303	283	302	-103
Short-term Savings (cumulative)			298	**-5**	278	580	477

Source: PNC Bank

In the above example, notice that the short-term cumulative savings, used to cover biweekly and monthly expenses, shows a deficit for the August 19th paycheck. Using this detailed by-paycheck budget, you can see in advance that adjustments need to be made. Perhaps you could eliminate entertainment for those two weeks, which presumably would also eliminate babysitting costs. Therefore, you would show a savings for that period, as well as meeting all your expenses for all paycheck periods.

Once you've started using your budget, monitor it regularly -- at first weekly, then whenever you pay bills. Even a good budget will need some adjustments now and then. For instance, food costs can quickly and easily get off track, due to either increased prices or unplanned purchases. Regularly monitoring your budget allows you to adjust your food costs (*see Food*).

To help recognize necessary adjustments, add Actual columns to your budget sheet for every paycheck period, and enter the actual expenses:

Paycheck Budget

(paid every two weeks)

Paydates (with Net Income shown in the square below)

Item	Amt.	Due	5-Aug	Actual	19-Aug	Actual
Every pay items:			$ 1,047	$ 1,047	$ 1,047	$ 1,047
Grocery store	$ 80	every	80	**90**	80	80
Eating out	$ 20	every	20	**30**	50	20
Transportation	$ 50	every	50	50	50	50
401K Retirement	$ 80	every	80	80	80	80
Long-term Savings	$ 25	every	25	25	25	25
Church ($5/wk)	$ 10	every	10	10	10	10
Entertainment	$ 30	every	30	30	30	30
Babysitting	$ 40	every	40	40	40	40
Monthly items:						
Rent/mortgage	$ 600	1st			600	600
Electric	$ 100	1st			100	100
Heat	$ 100	1st			100	100
Phone	$ 30	15th	30	30		
Car payment	$ 250	15th	250	250		
Credit card 1	$ 50	15th	50	50		
Credit card 2	$ 50	20th		50	50	50
Cable TV	$ 54	15th	54	54		
Finance fees	$ 6	20th		6	6	6
Other regular items:						
Hair	$ 15	3wks		15	15	15
Car insurance	$ 200	6 mos				
Tenants insurance	$ 120	6 mos				
Occasional items:						
Clothes	$ 30	per mo	30	30		
Furnishings	$ 10	per mo			10	10
Gifts	$ 300	per yr			24	24
Vacation	?	per yr				
Repairs		as needed				
Total Expenses			749	**840**	1270	1240
Difference (Income-Expenses)			298	**207**	-223	-193
Short-term Savings (cumulative)			298	**207**	75	14

In the above example, food and eating out exceeded budget, thereby reducing the short-term cumulative savings. Recognizing this can help you correct your budget before the next paycheck, perhaps by eliminating eating out or entertainment next pay period.

Food isn't the only place for savings. Here are some other ideas for keeping your budget on track:

1. Review your habits; perhaps you can do with a more basic cable plan or without caller ID. Do you pay full price at a convenience store for items you could buy for less on your weekly grocery shopping trips?

2. Some people fritter away cash; others use a debit card as if it had unlimited credit. Whichever you might be, consider converting; for example, a debit card user is more likely to think twice about spending cash, especially if he/she leaves the ATM card at home.

3. If things still aren't adding up, look at whether you need to adjust your allocations, change your spending habits, and/or increase your income (See *"5 steps to fix a broken budget"*).

Successful budgeting takes time and practice. Don't be discouraged if you don't hit your monthly goals at first. Following are some ideas to make it easier:

- Write it down so you're more likely stick to it.

- Change spending habits one or two categories at a time; e.g., track groceries and utilities for a month, analyze those expenses, then move on to personal care and entertainment spending, and so forth.

- When you get an "extra" paycheck or a bonus, save it or use it to pay down debt – or both.

- If you can't spend less, increase your income by selling unnecessary items or working a second part-time job.

- Think ahead. If you know your situation is going to change -a new baby, a necessary new appliance – plan and save for it, and try to pay cash.

- Keep spending "mistakes" in perspective – we all make them.

- As your income climbs, don't splurge until you're sure you're staying ahead of inflation. First, add the additional money to your retirement savings; since you didn't have it before, you won't miss it. Once you're sure you're staying ahead of inflation, if you want to allocate some of the additional income to other expenditures, you can. A good budget grows with you, so it's worth re-evaluating your budget every year.

5 steps to fix a broken budget

1. *Purpose:* Budgets often fail because they lack a sense of purpose. That purpose will be your mainstay and reference for every spending decision. The purpose of being financially independent and sound in your retirement years is an admirable one. Keep this purpose in mind every day to help conquer your spending temptations, and it will serve you well in the long run.

2. *Tracking:* After a while, many people fail to continue to track their expenses. Major life changes, such as illness, a job change, or a new home, can cause a hiatus from monitoring our cash flow. Record keeping, via paper, computer, or whatever, is very important, especially in the beginning when there's a tendency to think that spending $5 here or there doesn't matter. We need to keep expense tracking front and center at all times.

3. *Timing:* Your budget is more likely to fail if you tighten your belt too quickly. If you want to save $200 a month, try saving $50 in a week first. Decide on a target amount to maintain or to trim in each category, depending on your goals.

4. *Method:* Successful budgeters agree that a workable budget is one that fits your lifestyle and personality as well as your money. A macro method is based on covering the big chunks -- living expenses, savings, retirement -- and leaving the remaining cash to your own discretion. The 60% Solution is such a macro plan. A micro method is based on adjusting individual budget categories, transferring cash between categories as needed. The envelope system -- where you spend only the cash available in each envelope -- is a micro plan. An added element to a micro budget is timing expenses to each paycheck, paying one set of bills and setting aside savings with the first paycheck of the month, and then paying rent and smaller bills with the second. If you get 26 paychecks a year, the "extra" paychecks can go straight to your retirement fund.

5. *Flexibility:* A good budget can adjust to your changing needs as your life changes. A macro method like the 60% Solution can do this by allowing you to allocate 10% of your gross income to short-term savings to cover life's contingencies, and 10% to long-term savings. Using a micro method, you can adjust one category to provide cash for another. Whichever method you use, a good spending plan is and will always be a work in progress.

Credit/Debt

In some cases, such as when you're uninsured and trying to get medical care, using a credit card can seem the only way out. However, it's still your responsibility to deal with this debt. It's up to you to figure out how to live on what you make. There are undoubtedly families bigger than yours living on less and doing it without going into debt. Normally, if you can't pay your bill in full, stop using credit, pay far more than the minimum, and come up with a plan for paying it off entirely before you pick up the cards again.

- *Anytime you consider a loan, bring a calculator* so you can get the real cost of what you're buying by multiplying the payment by the number of months you'll be paying.

- *Use shredded credit card invitations to mulch your garden.* What a great way to put junk mail to good use!

- *Don't carry a balance on your credit cards*; pay the entire balance when due.

- *Don't pay interest on anything that loses value,* such as groceries or gas.

- *Pay down debt.* Do what you can to reduce your debt, particularly credit card debt, as much as possible to free up some monthly cash flow for savings, especially during a recession. If it's not realistic to pay it all off immediately, pay off maxed-out cards first (maxing out cards hurts your credit scores and can result in additional penalty rates and fees), then pay the card with the highest interest rate to avoid future charges.

- *If possible, transfer all your debt to a credit card with a lower interest rate.* Rates normally decrease during a recession. Watch out for introductory offers; don't get hooked by the promise of a 5% rate only to find that it'll increase to 18% after three or six months, unless you're confident you can pay off the entire balance within the introductory period. Also, a low-rate card with an annual fee may not be such a great deal; for instance, if you pay $40 a month toward a $1,000 balance on a card with a 12% interest rate and a $50 annual fee, that's equivalent to a no-fee card with an 18.4% interest rate.

- *If you transfer a balance, don't make further charges to that card if at all possible,* since those charges may incur a much higher interest rate. Also, payments will typically apply first to more recent charges so that your original transferred balance doesn't get reduced. Again, check the fine print – some cards offer 0% or a low interest rate for their introductory period, but if the balance isn't completely paid off in time, you'll be charged the accumulated interest on the entire original balance at the end of that period.

- *Negotiate your rates.* Credit card companies will regularly raise your rates if they can get away with it, so you have to frequently monitor those rates. Call your credit card company or bank and request a lower rate. If you have good credit, the lender might consider it. You'll have a stronger case if you can give examples of offers you've received from other companies.

- *Negotiate student loans.* If you're having trouble making your student loan payments, contact your lender for more affordable payment options. Many offer income-contingent or graduated payment options, and you may be able to get a deferral or forbearance if you're in dire straits.

- *Lower mortgage and car loan payments.* If your mortgage or car loan payments are too high, your options are more limited, but some lenders may offer to lower your payments, or you may be able to refinance to a lower rate if you have sufficient equity.

- *Set up automatic payments to pay off the bill.* Making the payments automatic helps to prevent our tendency to put off doing what's best, including paying off our debts.

- *Use rewards credit cards.* If you already pay off your balances in full every month, look for cards that give you cash back or rewards equal to 1.5% or more of your spending.

- *Stay aware of your credit ratings.* You're legally entitled to one free credit report once a year from each of the three main credit bureaus. Go to AnnualCreditReport.com to see what lenders see about your credit history.

- *Cut up your credit cards and deal only in cash.*

Desperate times can result in desperate decisions. If a solution sounds too good to be true, it usually is. The words 'quick and easy' should immediately raise a red flag. During a downturned economy that spawns such desperate measures as bankruptcies and foreclosures, businesses that thrive on consumers' desperation and desire for a quick fix abound.

Following are some "quick fixes" to avoid:

1. ***Paycheck loans -*** Writing a postdated check to a paycheck lender for $300 and getting $255 in cash may seem like a quick and easy fix. That $45 fee may not seem like much, but for a two-week loan it represents an annual interest rate of about 400%.

   Even worse, one paycheck loan may turn into a cycle of borrowing that can quickly grow to a huge debt. You'll most likely run out of money again before the next payday, especially since you now have to pay back that $300 loan.

   Soon, you may be borrowing from one paycheck lender to pay off another and so on ad infinitum. If you were managing your money well, you'd have an emergency fund or much cheaper credit available to you.

In the long run, you want to build a cash cushion (*see emergency fund*). Meanwhile, there are plenty of alternatives for dealing with a true emergency:

Ask your employer for an advance; some companies will give you part of your check early.

If you don't belong to a credit union, check out FindaCreditUnion.com. Not-for-profit credit unions have come up with alternatives to paycheck lenders, including short-term loans.

Sell off your unused and/or unneeded items; hold a garage or yard sale, or use online sites such as E-Bay.

As a last resort alternative to borrowing against your paycheck, you could get a cash advance on your credit card if you have available credit. This is a very expensive option; cash advances usually accrue at a much higher interest rate than other credit card debt -- typically well over 20%. But, as a last resort that's a bargain compared with a paycheck loan.

2. ***Car title loans*** - Title loans are like paycheck loans -- they come with triple-digit interest rates and short payback periods (usually one month), so many borrowers wind up "renewing" the debt over and over, often paying far more in fees than they initially borrowed. Moreover, if you fail to pay, the lender can take your car. If that's your only transportation to your job, you could quickly have an even bigger financial disaster -- no car and no job. If you have substantial equity in your car, you may be able to sell it, buy something cheaper and use the difference to meet your cash needs. If that's not a good option for you, explore the alternatives mentioned above regarding paycheck loans.

3. ***Debt settlement*** - Debt-settlement companies who promise they can get you out of debt cheaply typically have you stop paying your creditors and send the money to them instead. They assume that after a few months of not getting paid, your creditors will agree to a fraction of what they're owed. The settlement company says they'll then negotiate with your lenders and use the money you've sent to pay them.

By then, your credit will be destroyed, you'll have paid inordinate fees to the debt-settlement company, and you may be facing lawsuits from your lenders. Or worse, the debt-settlement company will disappear with your money. Some alternatives are:

a. Legitimate credit counselors who have debt-management plans that reduce or eliminate interest rates on your credit cards. Find one by visiting the http://www.nfcc.org/, the Web site of the National Foundation for Credit Counseling.

Note: Credit counseling may have implications for your credit rating, but the effect is far less than if you don't try to settle your debts.

b. Bankruptcy - if you can't pay your debts, you may be better off filing for bankruptcy, if you qualify. Your credit rating may recover more quickly, and you'll be able to keep the cash you would have spent on debt settlement. Consult an experienced bankruptcy attorney and discuss your options. A good source of information and resources is MSN Money's bankruptcy guide.

4. ***Debt-consolidation loans from private lenders*** - If you owe money to lots of creditors, you may get the promise from debt consolidators to combine all your debts into one "affordable" loan. These loans often come with high interest rates and hidden fees. Instead of helping you pay your debt off faster, a debt-consolidation loan can stretch out your repayment schedule so you actually end up paying more.

Some alternatives are:

a. Do it yourself - Try negotiating lower interest rates on your debt yourself. Some creditors would rather work with you than see the debt go unpaid. Then, handle your bills one at a time, starting with the highest rate debt or the credit card that's closest to its limit, while paying the minimums on your other debt. Once this high-priority debt is paid off, make the same-sized payment to the next highest priority debt. Continue until you're debt free.

b. A debt consolidation loan from a credit union - Credit unions tend to offer more reasonable interest rates.

c. Credit counseling - If you can't afford to make the minimum payments on the debt you have, a credit counselor might be your best option. (*See credit counselors*)

d. A home-equity loan - Consider this option only if you have plenty of equity in your home, you stop the behavior that got you into debt in the first place, and you pay off the loan as quickly as possible. Otherwise, you'll just be draining one of your most important assets, and you'll wind up deeper in debt. A regular home-equity loan is generally the best choice when you know exactly how much your purchase is likely to cost and you need several years to pay it off; for example, a major home-improvement project. A home equity line of credit may be a better option for shorter-term borrowing, or when you want to be able to tap your home equity to cover emergencies.

e.   A line of credit works more like a credit card, and has variable interest rates that are tied to the prime rate. A home equity line of credit is relatively inexpensive to have and to use. HELOCs typically cost nothing to set up, and most have relatively low annual fees ($50 to $100 is typical). The interest rate is low, and you don't have to pay any principal during the first 10 years or so. So if your interest rate is 7%, you can take about $70 of every $1,000 you borrow and use it to make your payments until the crunch passes.

5. ***Debt elimination*** - People who promise you debt elimination are con artists; they want you to believe that you can legally erase your debt with documents you purchase from them for a substantial fee.

6. ***Retirement plan withdrawals*** - You'll pay penalties and taxes on any withdrawal. Worse, you'll lose all future tax-deferred returns that money could have earned. If you're 30 years from retirement, every $10,000 withdrawal costs you at least $100,000 in lost future retirement income, assuming at least an 8% average annual return. The younger you are, the worse it is -- someone 40 years from retirement would lose more than $200,000 for each premature $10,000 withdrawal. Some alternatives:

7. ***Retirement plan loans*** - These are not risk-free, but they're better than withdrawals. Most workplace plans, including 401ks and 403bs, allow you to borrow up to half your balance or $50,000, whichever is less. Typically, you pay the money back over five years. Keep in mind that if you lose your job and can't pay back the loan, it becomes a withdrawal -- with taxes, penalties and the lost returns you were trying to avoid.

In general, leave your retirement accounts for retirement.

You can usually find a better solution to your money problems than raiding your future.

Credit card charges to avoid:

Sometimes you can't avoid using a credit card when you're strapped; but before you do, consider other options for warding off financial disaster:

- ***Extra fees*** - If a transaction requires you to pay extra to use a card, such as a cash advance, it's typically not worth it.

- ***Necessities*** - Don't charge necessities like groceries or regular bills, or anything you can't pay for in full when the bill arrives. If crunch time has come and you're tempted to charge necessities, here's what you need to do:

    - Cut your expenses to the bone before charging them; for example, reduce or shut off the cable service, cook your meals, get a bus pass; review every expense and cut until it hurts. *(See Trimming Expenses)*

    - Get your rates as low as possible. If you have good credit, your credit card interest rate should be below 10%, according to Curtis Arnold, the author of "How You Can Profit from Credit Cards." Lower your rates even more by using balance transfer offers or asking your issuer for a more competitive rate.

    - Understand there may be credit fallout. Many credit card companies use a program that flags users if they suddenly start charging more necessities and taking out cash advances. Such behavior can indicate a greater risk. The issuer may raise your rate, lower your limit, or take other steps to reduce its exposure.

    – Take advantage of available help. Refer to GovBenefits.gov. This federal government site has an interactive tool that can help you identify aid programs you might be eligible for, as well as links that can connect you to state resources. Also, try your state Human Services agency. When it comes down to choosing between charging groceries you can't afford and using food stamps, use the stamps.

- ***Taxes*** - You might even be tempted to charge your tax bill if you don't have the cash handy, or if you have a rewards credit card and want the frequent-flier miles, cash back or other goodies.

    Many government tax agencies, including the Internal Revenue Service, now accept credit card payments. However, these transactions are usually arranged through middlemen who charge a 2.49% "convenience fee." That fee wipes out any benefit from most credit cards, which offer rewards typically worth 1% to 2% of the amount charged. If you carry a balance, it quickly gets worse. For example, if you charged a $2,000 tax bill to a card with a 13% interest rate and paid only the monthly minimum (probably $40 at first and dropping over time), it would take you something like 20 years to pay it off and cost nearly $2,000 in interest.

    If you're likely to owe this debt for a while, you're probably better off making payment arrangements with the tax authority.

    The IRS currently charges a 7% interest rate for payment plans that last up to five years. If you can pay off the bill in less than a year and don't want to arrange an IRS payment plan, a credit card payment may be feasible if you handle the transaction carefully. Get the best deal, and make sure you arrange automatic payments to pay off the debt as quickly as possible.

To avoid this situation in the future, adjust your withholding. The IRS has a calculator on its Web site. If you run your own business or otherwise have a complicated tax situation, hire a professional.

- ***Preventive maintenance:*** Emergency fund *(See emergency)*. Even though it may take you a while to build one while you work on other priorities -- saving for retirement, paying off debt -- you still should save an amount equal to three months' expenses, preferably six months', as soon as you can.

Three things you should never charge are your mortgage, car note, or student loan. These lenders typically don't accept plastic directly. A company called ChargeSmart now offers credit card users the option to charge many mortgage, auto loan, student loan or utility payments. The cost is $4.95 plus 2.29% of the transaction amount. This fee usually wipes out any benefit your rewards card might offer, and carrying that balance on your credit card increases the costs.

If you're in over your head with student loans, ask your lender if you qualify for a graduated payment schedule (your payments start out small and increase as, presumably, your income increases), or ask for an extended payment period, such as 15 or 20 years.

If you don't have the cash to pay your bill, ask yourself this:

"Is this a one-time event, or am I just putting off the inevitable?"

Ideally, you have some emergency savings to help you with unexpected expenses. If you don't, then borrowing money to pay your mortgage or other loans may not be a disaster, as long as the need is short-lived.

If you've been without a job for months, if your mortgage payment is more than 30% of your gross income, or if your car expenses exceed 10% of your gross income, your problems are more than temporary. Borrowing any more will just add to the problems. It's time to get your expenses in line with your income, even if that means drastic changes such as moving or selling your car.

Speed Up Your Debt Payments
Without Sending More Money

A credit card typically compounds interest daily (*See compounded interest*). So it makes sense that paying frequently actually saves on interest. You can continue sending the same exact amount to your credit card bill each month; but, send it in two payments and you'll save on the amount of interest you are paying, which means more of your payment is going towards the balance and less towards interest.

Accounts other than credit card accounts where you can really make a difference just by dividing your payments in half and sending them twice a month include car loans and mortgages. You can save about 30% by making your mortgage payment twice a month rather than once a month, but be sure that your mortgage doesn't have a clause for prepayment penalties.

Protecting Your Credit

Great credit is a powerful weapon in a struggling economy. Here are some strategies for preserving yours:

Know what's important to your credit scores - You want your credit scores, the three-digit numbers lenders use to gauge your creditworthiness, to be as high as possible. Credit is still freely available to those with good scores, usually 720 or above.

Credit information is important in other ways as well. Insurance companies, employers and landlords use credit reports to evaluate applications. Good scores will help keep your premiums down, qualify you for jobs involving money and land you better places to live.

Here are the essentials of credit scoring:

1. *Pay your bills on time.* A single skipped payment can knock 100 points off your FICO scores, the ones most used by lenders. Consider automatic payments and e-mail alerts to make sure you don't forget to pay a bill.

2. *Pay down your debts.* Most importantly, keep your credit card balances low relative to your credit limits. Try to use no more than 30% of your credit limits; 10% or less is even better.

3. *Beware of opening or closing accounts.* Either can hurt your scores.

4. *Dispute any serious credit report errors.* Dispute any accounts that aren't yours or negative information that should have been deleted. (Most negatives, such as late payments or charge-offs, should be dropped after seven years. Bankruptcies can stay on for up to 10 years; unpaid tax liens may be reported indefinitely.)

Monitor your credit reports - Although reporting false information to the credit bureaus is illegal, bogus collections do wind up on credit reports all the time. As the economy worsens, this happens more often as lenders sell off their debts to collectors, whose first action is often putting the account on your credit reports whether you owe the debt or not. You need to keep an eye on your reports so you can dispute such errors if they show up.

There's no need to pay for expensive credit monitoring services unless you're at high risk of becoming an identity theft victim. You're entitled to one free credit report per year from each of the three credit bureaus. You can adequately monitor your reports by requesting a different bureau's report every four months from the free, federally mandated site AnnualCreditReport.com. You might request your report from Experian this month, for example, then your report from TransUnion in four months, then your report from Equifax four months later, and then start all over again.

Monitor your medical bills - Rather than try to collect on bills themselves, more medical providers are turning unpaid accounts over to collection agencies, which promptly report the debts to the credit bureaus. Because even a small collection account can do serious damage to your scores, you want to prevent a bill from reaching this stage if possible. If you have health insurance, follow up on every medical bill to ensure it gets paid and that any disputes are worked out. If a bill goes unpaid for more than a few months, call the billing office of the medical provider and let them know you're working on a resolution. Make sure the billing office has your correct contact information and ask it not to turn the bill over to collections while the dispute is being resolved. If you don't have insurance, try to negotiate a discounted bill and/ or work out a payment plan.

Keep your credit options open - The best advice is to not carry credit card balances, keep old credit card accounts available, and have cards from at least two different issuers to maximize your flexibility.

Carrying credit card debt is always a bad idea but is especially so during a recession. Credit card companies are managing their costs aggressively, which means they're jacking up interest rates on some customers with little warning or justification. Higher rates make it tougher to repay the debt, and increase your chances of falling behind. Issuers also are lowering credit limits or shutting down some accounts entirely, either because the borrower has been deemed too risky or because the account hasn't been used in recent months. Lower limits and closed accounts can hurt your credit scores.

- *Transfer high-rate balances if you can.* If you do carry a balance and your rate has skyrocketed or your credit limit has been lowered, check to see whether another of your cards has a low-rate balance transfer offer you can use (See *transferring credit balances*). Use the low rate to help you pay off the debt; don't keep bouncing it from card to card.

- *Try to keep your oldest and highest-limit accounts active.* Accounts that aren't used cost issuers money, but shutting them down may hurt your credit scores and reduce your access to credit in an emergency. Charge some small amount to these accounts monthly; you can also have the balances automatically deducted from your checking account.

- *Have more than one credit card available.* Having access to a line of credit can help you survive a prolonged financial setback. Setting up a home equity line of credit may be a good strategy for you (See *home equity loans*). But, with lenders freezing some home-equity lines, credit cards may become your supplement to whatever emergency fund you've accumulated.

Conserve your cash - There's nothing like a big pile of savings to help you through a bad time. It's never too late to start accumulating one. Following are some ideas on where to find the money:

- *Use your income tax refund* and any stimulus rebate checks you get.

- *Fix your withholding* for the rest of the year so you get bigger paychecks; set up an automatic transfer to put the additional money into savings.

- *Stop making extra payments* on mortgages and student loans and funnel that money into savings. If you have a home-equity line of credit that may be frozen or trimmed, think twice about paying down the balance, because you may not be able to access that credit again in an emergency.

- *Host a yard sale* or sell stuff on eBay or Craigslist**.**

- *Get a second job.*

- *Trim your expenses* (See *Trimming Expenses*).

Be cautious about adding to your overhead - Every bill or debt you add now may be one you'll struggle to pay should you lose your job. Businesses desperate for sales will offer deep discounts and low-rate financing. Unless your job is rock solid, your emergency fund substantial and your expenses already low, you should resist the urge.

Have a Contingency Plan - If you lose your job or start struggling to pay your bills, here are some ways you can do to try to save your credit with different types of borrowing:

- *Contact your mortgage lender.* The earlier you act, the better your chances of avoiding late payments or a notice of default, the legal notice that starts the foreclosure process, which devastates your credit scores. Also contact a HUD-approved housing counselor – at www.hud.gov -- to review your situation and discuss your options.

- *Get a student loan forbearance or deferral.* You may be able to get a reprieve from payments, although interest typically continues to accrue (See *negotiate student loans*). Facing a bigger balance is better than defaulting, and the room this gives you can help you pay other bills.

- *Sell or refinance your car.* If your auto loan payments are too high, you might be able to refinance for a lower payment, if you have equity. Another option is to sell it and use the equity to pay cash for a cheaper car. If you owe more than the car is worth, you may be able to persuade a credit union to lend you money to make up the difference.

- *Deal with your credit cards.* If you're in danger of falling behind on your credit card payments, make an appointment with a legitimate credit counselor (See **credit counselors**). Credit counseling itself doesn't affect your FICO credit scores, although it may have other repercussions on your credit. Still, this is less severe and long-lasting than default, bankruptcy or debt settlement.

Saving

Following any one of these first ten tips can save you as much as $500 per year. For example, switch to U.S. Energy Star-approved light bulbs and save $60 a year; save more than $200 a year by turning off the TV when nobody's watching it (running a 32-inch TV four hours a day costs $3 per month); wash clothes in cold water for another $60 a year; power down your computer at night to save $70 a year. Total annual savings = $390 per year.

Some of these tips can save you even more. If you follow all 10, you'll save at least $5,000 a year:

1. Drive less.
2. Take your own beverages to work.
3. Conserve energy: lower the thermostat when heating and raise it when cooling, turn off the lights and TV when leaving a room, conserve water usage.
4. Garden.
5. Get small or no pets.
6. Buy no-name brands and, if possible, buy necessities in bulk.
7. Reduce TV, phone and Internet services/subscriptions to minimum necessities -- eliminate movie and sports channels, caller ID and call waiting, etc.
8. Sign up for tax-advantaged plans at work -- education, health, transportation and child-care savings accounts.
9. Eat in.
10. Pay credit card bills in full as soon as possible, and take advantage of free bill pay.

More tips:

11. Invest as much as possible to maximize company contributions in a 401K plan if your employer has one; if not, consider an IRA.

12. Look for banks with highest savings interest rates.

13. Keep your savings in a separate bank from your checking so it's a little more cumbersome to transfer savings money to your checking account.

14. Don't pay with coins, just pay with bills; then, save the pocket change daily. I have a battery-operated coin counter and wrapper, and each evening I just put all my loose change in it; once I've accumulated about $100 worth of wrapped coins, I take it to the bank and deposit it in my savings account. You'll be surprised at how quickly it adds up!

15. Forego charitable contributions unless you have money to spare; remember – "charity begins at home".

16. Keep any irregular income – commissions, bonuses, overtime, gifts, money found on the street -- in a separate account for emergencies, or add it to your regular savings account.

17. Save the first $1000-$1500 as quickly as possible for an emergency fund – keep it in a separate account; start by focusing on the first $500 cushion.

18. Keep an extra $100 in your checking account - maintain this cushion and don't spend it; this will lower your odds of bouncing a check. You can also sign up for overdraft protection for accidental overdrafts, if you have another account the bank can draw from; just be mindful of the associated fees. My bank charged a $10 or $20 upfront fee for the plan, then $10 per overdraft occurrence, whether it's one check or 10 checks that bounce during that occurrence. Some people write themselves a phony

check for their cushion amount to keep from spending it. When tracking your balance online or at an ATM, you'll need to mentally deduct the $100.

19. Build a $500 emergency savings account - $500 will cover a good portion of most real emergencies that crop up, such as car repairs, insurance deductibles, and replacing an appliance. Even if the unexpected expense is higher than $500, you'll be able to reduce the amount needed by that much. Some ideas for scraping up $500:

   – Use your tax refund - The typical refund check is more than $2,000, so most people will have enough even for a full $1500 emergency fund.

   – Sell - At yard sales, consignment stores, online auction sites like eBay, Amazon.com, classified sites like Craigslist. Be sure to put the cash in savings right away, or you'll end up spending it.

   – Save your change - At the end of each day, put all your coins in a jar or a battery-operated coin counter. This can result in hundreds of dollars by the end of a year. Encourage your children to do the same to teach them how to save.

   – Automatic transfers - Setting up a regular automatic electronic transfer from checking to savings account, rather than manually transferring the money, will eliminate the need for a conscious decision to save every month and reduce your chances of spending it. You can start with just $10 or $20 per paycheck; obviously the more you can live without, the faster you'll save the $500.

   – *Don't touch this emergency money unless it's a **real** emergency* - If you're in debt, you need to get out of the habit of looking for a quick "fix" when you experience unexpected expenses. If the spending is absolutely necessary, you're better off paying cash than paying interest on money borrowed from credit cards or lenders; afterward, you can concentrate on rebuilding your cushion as quickly as possible.

What constitutes a ***real*** emergency? Basically, it's an event that puts your livelihood or your family's safety at

risk. The TV dying is not an emergency; the furnace dying is an emergency.

A car repair may or may not be an emergency. If you have no alternative means of transportation to get to work, then getting the car fixed justifies raiding your emergency fund; if you can take the bus for a while or carpool with someone else, it doesn't.

– *College savings* - Saving for retirement is more important. Your child can get student loans, but no one will lend you money for retirement. But contributing even a small amount each month will help reduce the amount of debt your child eventually incurs, so try to put at least $25 a month per kid in a college savings plan. Thanks to recent tax law changes and reductions in fees, 529 college-savings plans have emerged as the best way for most parents to save.

Remember why you're saving

- Make a chart showing your debts and plot each month's payment so you can have visual evidence that your balances are going down.

- Keep your goal in mind to help you fight the urge to spend; even if you're already living frugally as a matter of survival, take pride in further improving your money management skills and congratulate yourself when you've made it through one month better than the last.

- Find support systems; use Internet sites and message boards devoted to frugal living, and spend time with people who support your goals. For example, have pot luck dinners -- at each others' homes -- with friends who are also focused on improving their financial situation.

Priorities:

1. Your highest priority should be saving for retirement; every dollar you don't save today costs you $10 or more in lost retirement income. The younger you are, the more you'll lose by not tucking money away now *(See Retirement)*. Take advantage of opportunities for a 401(k) match, or fund an IRA or Roth.

2. Dispatching credit card debt should be your next highest priority, since it's probably accumulating at double-digit interest rates and reducing your financial flexibility.

3. Finally, a cushion equal to three to six months' worth of expenses can be a defense against life's unexpected setbacks -- job loss, disability, illness, accidents, natural disasters. Having cash in a high-rate savings account can also do wonders for reducing your money anxieties.

Regardless of how much or how little you make, always save a little - Pay yourself first; whatever money you net, you can and should be saving some of it.

Food & Supplies

- *Cook at home*; don't eat out or take out, or at least do it infrequently.

- *If possible, change to a meatless diet* due to costs (be sure to check with your physician first).

- *Cook a lot of casseroles*, stews, and soups for meals that go further.

- *Plan two weeks' menus* in advance; cook the meal on weekends and freeze them in one-meal portions. This saves money (since you can buy in larger quantities), and time during the work week.

- *Bring your lunch to work.* Spending just $2 a day on a homemade lunch versus $6 a day on the sandwich shop will save about $80 a month, or $960 each year. Buy lunch meats (and cheeses) for two weeks' lunches, use half the first week; if you don't use them on the weekend or the next week, freeze the remainder until you're ready to use them again.

- *Take your own beverages to work,* or when going out for the day. Either bringing coffee from home or brewing it in the break room at work will cut costs dramatically; you can go from spending $500 a year or more to about $50. Save more by taking cans of soda or bottled water with you instead of buying them. You can go even further by cleaning your plastic water bottles and replenishing them with drinking water from your tap water or from a gallon jug. (It's an environmentally friendly move, too.)

Grocery Shopping

The average U.S. household spends 13% of its budget on food, but savvy supermarket shoppers can save hundreds of dollars a month. Because food is an essential, it sometimes goes unchallenged as a spending category in many people's budgets; it seems easier to cut back in other areas first -- clothes shopping, cable services, vacations and other extras. Combining coupons, rebates, store sales and a little effort can save you big bucks when shopping, without sacrificing quality. Here are some tips:

- *Get to know sales cycles.* Stores reduce their products according to a 12-week cycle. If your spaghetti sauce is normally $2.19 a jar; on sale it's $1.99. That's the "phantom sale price", so wait until the price drops to two for $3; but don't buy until it hits the rock-bottom price of, say, 10 for $10 or BOGO -- buy one, get one free. Keep a price notebook for a while so that you get to know the rock-bottom prices for most items. That way you're less likely to get sucked in by phantom sale prices because you know a steeper discount is coming.

- *Don't shop when you're hungry.* Grocery shopping when you're hungry will tempt you to stray from your list (see below). It leads to impulsive buying of more items, as well as more costly items.

- *Make fewer trips to the grocery store.* Making bigger shopping trips less often cuts down on impulse buys. Shoppers making a "quick trip" to a store usually purchase 54% more than they planned, according to a study published by the Marketing Science Institute. Going to a grocery store three times a week, and spending $10 on impulse buys each trip, adds up to $120 extra per month. If you go only once a week, you'll spend $40 per month on impulse buys, which saves $80 per month, or $960 per year. Also, don't pay full price at a convenience store for items you could buy for less on your weekly grocery shopping trips. To save even more, try grocery shopping only once every two weeks and only buy needed staples, like milk, in between trips.

- *Make a list beforehand and stick to it.* If you make a list of only items you need (factor in treats, snacks and lunches), and you don't stray from your list while shopping, you'll save money and time. The only exception would be if you spot a loss leader (see below). Leave off the grocery list things packaged for convenience, like the 100-calorie snack packs, puddings, baby carrots, cookies, crackers, etc.; the extra cost for the convenience packaging is far more than it's worth. You can portion and package these things yourself easily and cheaply after saving money by buying the larger packages. Some snacks that are healthful and dirt-cheap, and that you can snack-size package yourself are:
  - Raisins (from the big generic canister).
  - Popcorn (made on our stove popper, rather than in the microwave)
  - Carrot sticks
  - Pretzels
  - Cheese
  - Bananas
- *Stick to the perimeters of the supermarket.* Here you'll find all the unprocessed basics you need -- dairy products, meats, bread. Avoid inner aisles, which are intentionally filled with tempting processed foods that drain budgets.
- *Buy in season.* Make it a habit to eat what's in season locally. Don't buy strawberries in January. Guard against cravings by canning or freezing fresh items so you can enjoy those berries any time of year.
- *Buy in bulk when on sale* or at a good price (as long as it's on your list and you'll use it all), then freeze or can it. When buying in bulk, compare prices to those at a wholesaler, such as Wal-Mart, Costco, BJ's, or Sam's Club. Off-brand toilet paper, paper towels, tissues, paper

cups, plastic wrap, plastic bags, etc., are all available at half the price of similar name-brand products when you buy them in bulk. Buying big can be a tremendous deal and easily cut costs by $500 per year. But remember, putting these purchases on your credit card defeats the purpose. So, you need the cash and the storage space to fully take advantage of bulk buying.

- *Buy generic.* You can almost always save money by choosing a store brand or no-name brand, and you usually won't sacrifice quality on many items, including cereal, canned goods, and frozen vegetables. Also, the savings on generic baby formula and prescription drugs can be huge. However, sometimes brand names on sale are cheaper than store brand equivalents, so always comparison shop.

- *Spot the loss leaders.* Those are the staggering deals – Tropicana orange juice for a nickel -- that lure unsuspecting customers into stores, who then buy lots of other things they don't need. If you see an unbelievable deal, grab it; just don't buy anything else.

- *Become a coupon collector.* You can organize fliers by date, or by product type, in a hanging file kept in your car. But, don't just depend on fliers. Supermarkets place coupons at the front of the store and/or next to discounted items. Keep the coupons, even if you don't need the items right away. Also, ask friends to give you coupons they don't use. And, check out http://couponmom.com.

- *Subscribe to your Sunday newspaper.* If you're diligent with your coupon collecting, it will pay for the paper in no time.

- *Pay nothing.* If you have a $1 coupon for Suave shampoo, which is $1.99, and it's double coupon day, you can get it for free. But, learn the rules of each store by asking;

some won't double a coupon if doubling it exceeds the face value of the item.

- *Do the math.* There are times when buying two of an item in a smaller size will be cheaper than buying one larger size. It makes no sense, but stores make mistakes too. Comparison shop by unit price, not total price (per ounce, pound, etc.). For example, a pack of 40 diapers may cost $13, or 33 cents per diaper. A box of 144 diapers may cost $35, or 24 cents per diaper. A difference of 9 cents may not seem like much, but when you change a diaper six to eight times each day, that amounts to a savings of $16 to $22 per month.

  Note: Don't buy in bulk if you won't use it all; you're wasting your money, no matter how good a deal it is.

- *If an item is on sale,* say six for $3, don't assume you have to buy all six; you can often buy just one for the sale price of 50 cents.

- *Stand your financial ground.* Hostile checkout people sometimes try to sabotage your savings efforts. The only solution is to talk to a manager -- and be willing to wait in line.

- *Pay with cash.* You'll be more likely to stick to your shopping list.

Cooking and Saving

- *Use a crock pot or pressure cooker* to tenderize inexpensive and often tough cuts of meat. Microwave ovens, which most people tend to underutilize, also save time.

- *Consider adding at least three bean-based meals* to your week's menu, whether it's burritos, bean soup, or rice and beans.

- *Consider canned products,* such as salmon, tuna, chicken and clams, when the meat department is too expensive.

These are good in pasta and rice dishes, wraps, and casseroles.

- *Use canned fruit and frozen vegetables,* such as lima beans and peas, which are almost as nutritional. Even fresh produce is expensive these days;

- *Use regular plates and utensils.* Hand wash them or use the dishwasher, when fully loaded, to eliminate costly disposable paper plates and plastic utensils.

- *Get a used freezer* to stock up on discounted meat. Or, if you live in ranching country, consider buying a half- or quarter- beef right from the grower. It costs a lot less per pound, and grass-fed beef is leaner and tastier.

- *Eat smaller, more realistic portions, and chew longer.* Most of us these days are always in a hurry and tend to not chew long enough. You will more genuinely feel full, not stuffed, and it will save on excesses. It's also healthier for digestion.

- *Water down juices.* When you open a new bottle of juice, pour half in the old container and add about 1/4 - 1/2 container of water to each bottle. This makes each new bottle last longer, especially if you have children, and it dilutes the grams of sugar and calories per serving.

- *Avoid using the oven during the summer.* Ovens heat a house faster than any other appliance, adding to the strain on air conditioning systems. Plan meals that don't require baking, or bake in the late evening and microwave to heat the next night.

- *Cook cheaper meals.* Instead of serving individual portions of meat, use it to supplement larger portions of rice or pasta in affordable casseroles, stews, or soups. For other low-cost ideas, check out the Department of Agriculture's "Recipes and Tips for Healthy, Thrifty Meals."

Eating Out

- *Break your restaurant routine.* We are creatures of habit and convenience. Make an effort to cut back, such as dining out once or twice a month instead of once or twice a week. With $20 meals, this simple act will trim your expenses by more than $100 a month. Also, consider eating out for lunch instead of dinner. That way, you can get lunch-menu prices for dinner-quality entrees.

- *Use coupons.* You know about coupons for groceries, but don't overlook bargains for dining out. For instance, at Restaurant.com you can get a $25 gift certificate to local restaurants for only $10. Check the coupon flyers and packs that come in the mail for restaurant bargains. Or, before you dine out check some websites, such as RetailMeNot.com, where you can quickly find printable coupons and codes for dozens of restaurants. You can also pick up a restaurant guide or a tour book of your city for budget-friendly suggestions; cutting just $5 from each meal bill is a savings.

- *When eating out, divide entrees in half and save the rest for a second meal.* Ask for a to-go box **as soon as your meal arrives** and save half for tomorrow's lunch or dinner. Restaurants are notorious these days for extra large portions, so this will help you spread out the calories and the cost of the meal.

- *Say no to fast food.* Unless you hit the dollar menu exclusively, fast food can add up in a hurry. Compare the cost of a combo meal for four people to sandwiches, chips and drinks from home.

Housing

Buying a house is an exciting prospect. But no matter how much you may want to own your own home, you need to realistically look at whether or not you can yet afford to. Following are some considerations:

- *Calculate the percentage of income.* If your mortgage or rent payment equals more than 30% of your gross income, you'll have a tough time paying the rest of your monthly bills.

- *If you can't afford to buy the house with a 30-year fixed-rate mortgage, you can't afford the house.* Don't finance with an adjustable-rate mortgage (ARM). This loan can immediately soar to a much higher interest rate. There are good reasons for choosing less traditional loans, but buying a house you couldn't otherwise afford isn't one of them. Too many people today are facing foreclosure because they used an adjustable or interest-only loan to buy too much house for their means. Read "Who's at most risk for foreclosure?" at MSN Money on MSN.com for the grim details.

- *Fix the rate for at least as long as you plan to be in the home.* Lenders, brokers or real-estate agents may tout the low payments of adjustable-rate loans, but in short time those payments will jump substantially. Protect your family and your investment by choosing a loan with a fixed-rate period that matches how long you expect to live there. If you're sure you'll move in five years, a five-year hybrid may be a good option. If you think you'll stay put for 10 years or more, you might just want the certainty of the 30-year fixed.

- *You have better things to do with your money than prepay a low-rate, deductible mortgage.* People get excited about how much interest they'll save by making additional mortgage payments. However, you can get a much better return elsewhere. Don't consider prepaying your mortgage until you're taking full advantage of your retirement savings options and have paid off all your other debt. For more details, read "Don't rush to pay off that mortgage" at MSN Money on MSN.com.

Insurance

- *Cover yourself for catastrophic expenses, not what you can cover out of pocket.* Insurance isn't meant to cover the normal expenses of daily living; it's designed to help you when expenses are so big they might otherwise wipe you out financially. Therefore, depending on your situation and what you're insuring, you may want high limits on your policies and high deductibles too. For more, read "3 costly myths about insurance." at MSN Money on MSN.com.

- *Those who need life insurance typically need five to 10 times their income.* Most people need to answer only two questions about insurance: "Do I need it?" and, if the answer is yes, "How much do I need?" You probably need life insurance if other people are financially dependent on you. If you're single or your children are grown, you probably don't need it. If you do need life insurance, be sure to buy enough. Term or "pure" insurance is usually the way to go. Insurance that includes an investment component, such as some annuities, can be as much as 10 times more costly and can devastate most families' budgets. The five- to 10-times-income rule is a pretty broad guideline, so you'll want to use MSN Money's (at MSN.com) Life Insurance Needs Estimator for a more precise indicator.

- *Raise car insurance deductibles.* Assuming you have a proper emergency fund in place, raise deductibles on insurance policies. The difference in a $500 deductible and a $1,000 deductible on your car insurance policy can help reduce your monthly or semi-annual premiums.

Phone, Internet and TV

- *Give up phone extras.* If you don't really need Caller ID, Call Waiting, Voice Mail, or internet service on your cell phone, drop one or all of them to save $5 to $50 each month.

- *Get a calling card.* Calling cards may save you money over the long distance plan offered by your phone company. For example, you can buy a phone card at a wholesale store like Costco with 700 prepaid minutes for $20. That's 2.9 cents per minute. A calling card may also help you better "budget" your long distance calls.

- *Prepay for your cell phone service.* The average wireless phone user spends about $60 a month, including taxes and fees. If you talk for 200 or fewer minutes per month, you may save by switching to a prepaid plan charging 25 cents a minute or less. Prepaid plans generally charge 10 cents to 60 cents a minute, and compatible phones cost as little as $20. For a more full-fledged plan, you may want to join a family plan with family or friends, sharing the minutes and apportioning the cost. This results in savings for everyone in the plan.

- *Eliminate your land line phone.* If you have a good cell phone plan that you use almost exclusively, get rid of duplicate costs by dropping your land line service. This could save you $20 to $50 or more each month.

- *Consider bundles.* For about $100 a month, you can get cable or satellite TV, local and long-distance telephone service, plus high-speed Internet service. This is often cheaper than paying for each service separately. Additionally, you pay just one bill, and you have just one company to call if you have an issue.

- *Rethink your phone company.* Save on your long distance bill and chat via computer with free software, like Skype.com.

You won't pay a dime for any call to another Skype user. You can call nonusers' landlines, too, for a nominal monthly fee (currently about $3). It sure beats the cost of a typical land line service. You may also want to consider other low-cost Internet phone services, such as Vonage. It comes with additional perks such as voice mail, caller ID and call waiting and costs $25 per month for free unlimited local and long-distance calls.

- *Evaluate your cable use.* Monitor what cable channels your family really uses and what you're paying for, then trim your cable costs accordingly. For instance, drop premium channels and any other unwatched channels you're paying extra for. If you watch movies or HBO series now and then, rent them. Blockbuster's online plan allows you to use the mail-in service and exchange at their store (the store will then do the mailing for you). This means you're getting two movies for the price of one, which cuts the cost in half. If you don't even watch TV enough to justify the cost of cable service, consider dropping cable entirely.

- *Negotiate a lower rate.* With cutthroat competition among phone, cable and Internet providers, you can probably haggle your way to a better deal on your service. Many of the best offers are for new customers, but that shouldn't stop you from asking for the same deal, or at least one better than what you're getting, especially if you can threaten to take your business elsewhere.

Utilities

- *Turn off the TV.* Running a 32-inch TV four hours a day costs $3 per month, but many families use the TV for background noise. You can save more than $200 a year just by turning off the TV when nobody's watching it.

- *Power down your computer* at night to save $70.

- *Check electrical wiring.* Be sure electrical wiring is sufficient and efficient enough for your household use to prevent costly over usage of electricity and to avoid safety hazards.

- *Turn off lights* when leaving a room to conserve electricity and reduce cost.

- *Replace light bulbs* with CFLs, compact fluorescent lights. Look for ones with a Kelvin temperature of 2,600 to 3,000. These lights not only last 10 times longer than incandescents but also save up to $60 in electricity per light over their lifetime.

- *Install occupancy sensors or timers* on lights in areas you use only occasionally and for exterior lights, which tend to get left on during the day. Anyone with basic wiring skills can install them.

- *Use power strips.* Of the total energy used to run home electronics, 40% is consumed when the appliances are turned off. Reduce this power drain by unplugging devices, or plugging them into a central power strip which can be powered down with the flip of a switch. You can also buy a device, such as a Smart Power Strip, which will automatically stop drawing electricity when the gadgets are off.

- *Use air conditioning and heating only when necessary* and as little as possible. Wear less or more clothing, such as sweaters and socks, depending on the season. Adjust the thermostat during the night and when away from the house for any length of time during the day, such as at work. For every degree you lower your home's temperature during the heating season, or raise it for air conditioning, subtract 5% from your bill.[10] An Energy Star programmable thermostat saves more than twice its price within a year and will adjust the temperature automatically.

- *Replace your air conditioner filter* every month when in use. Even though manufacturers suggest changing the filter every 90 days, systems work better when changed once a month, especially in peak times like summer. Instead of picking up a top-of-the-line air filter, go for a medium grade filter and just buy more of them.

- *Plant a tree next to your outside air conditioning unit.* By shading the unit you may improve the operating efficiency of the overall system by 20%. To maintain proper airflow, take care not to plant too close to the unit.

- *Have your furnace tuned* every two years to save about 10% on your heating bills.

- *Keep windows and doors well insulated* to preserve heat in the winter and cool air in the summer. Put weather strip around the frames of your front and back doors and save about $30 per year in energy costs.

- *Lower your water heater temperature* to 120°F. If your heater doesn't have a temperature gauge, dial down until the water feels hot but not scalding (before going too low, make sure your dishwasher has a booster heater, which gets the temperature up to the 140 degrees necessary for proper cleaning). Also, if you have a water heater built before 2004, wrap it in an insulating jacket such to save 10% (about $30) annually on your water-heating bill.

- *Forget baths; take showers instead.* Install a low-flow shower head that restricts the water output to as low as

1.5 gallons per minute, vs. 5.5 gpm, saving 7,300 gallons and $30-$100 a year. These usually cost $10-$20 and screw into existing fittings.

- *Fix water leaks.* A leaky faucet wastes as much as 2,700 gallons a year. Also, test toilets for leaks. Put a drop of food coloring in the toilet tank; if the color shows up in the bowl, your tank is leaking, and you're wasting up to 200 gallons of water a day.

- *Consider faucet aerators* that screw into your faucet threading and cut the water flow from 3-4 gallons per minute to as little as a half-gallon. Aerators blend water and air, reducing the flow without sacrificing pressure, and they only cost 50¢ to $3 apiece. A faucet that flows at 1 gpm is fine for the bathroom; but use an aerator with a flow rate of at least 2 gpm for the kitchen.

- *Do laundry only when you have a full load.* Use cold water to wash your clothes and save 50% of the energy you'd use for hot water.

- *Set your dryer on the moisture sensor*, not the timer, and cut energy use by another 15%.

- *Clean your clothes dryer filter* every time you dry a load, either before or after but stick to a regular routine; also remember to clean the dryer vent and vent hose occasionally to keep the dryer running more energy-efficient and prevent fires.

- *Run your dishwasher only for a full load.* Most energy used by dishwashers is to heat a set amount of water, so running smaller loads wastes both energy and water. Turn off the dishwasher before or part way into the dry cycle, open the door and pull out the racks to let the dishes air dry for more savings. If you don't have an automatic dishwasher, don't keep water running for rinsing while you're busy washing; fill a sink or dishpan with soapy water for washing, and use a second sink or dishpan filled with rinse water.

- *Keep the refrigerator coils clean;* pull the plug and vacuum the coils once every month or two.

- *Do routine maintenance tasks around your home.* Change the furnace filter, maintain fireplaces, change smoke alarm batteries twice a year (it's easier to remember if you make a habit of changing them when we turn the clocks ahead or back).

- *Water your outdoor plants in the early morning,* before the sun can burn off moisture, and take care not to overwater. Before starting your sprinkler, step on the grass. If the blades spring back, hold off watering for a day or two; the average lawn only needs an hour of watering a week. Also, raise your mower blades to the 3-inch setting. Shaggy grass holds moisture longer, requiring less watering.

- *Consider installing a drip irrigation system*, which maintains moisture in the soil. A drip system consists of a tube or hose with holes or emitters along it. It maintains the moisture level of the soil and uses a timer to deliver water to plants. Drip irrigation, compared to hand watering or sprinkler systems, can reduce water loss by 50%-60%.

10 Alliance to Save Energy

Entertainment

Even the tightest budget needs a little give, or the whole thing is likely to collapse. Enjoying life doesn't have to cost a lot, or anything at all. Some people tie their treats to specific goals, such as paying off a credit card. Others build in a little "splurge money," sometimes as little as $5 to $10 a month, to waste as they please.

- *Read through your community calendar* for cheap or free activities.
- *Have a picnic in the park.*
- *Enjoy an ice cream cone.*
- *Buy a small bunch of flowers* to spruce up your home.
- *Change your routine,* such as eating something besides chicken, or getting out of the house once in awhile.
- *Explore your city* for parks and playgrounds, museums, and historic sites.
- *Live in the moment.* Focusing on what you don't have is a recipe for discontent. Instead, concentrate on what you do have. For instance, rather than worry about not being able to buy a house, "practice" on your current home with redecorating projects, such as rearranging furniture, painting some furniture, and making repairs that have been put off.
- *Maintain an attitude of gratitude.* Keep a list of things you can be grateful for, and share it with family and friends.
- *Spend more time with friends and family,* a major benefit of frugal living. Share "theme nights":
    - Movie night, with 99-cent or online rentals
    - Baseball night (either playing or watching)
    - Game night
    - Water gun night

- *Volunteer.* Not only will you be breaking out of your routine but you'll be helping others.

- *Catch a matinee.* You can often get cheap tickets to movies, theater productions and other shows if you attend in the afternoon instead of the evening. Daytime is also a good time to try out a new restaurant; you may get lunch menu prices for dinner-quality entrees.

- *Watch for discount days*; many theaters, museums, galleries, zoos and parks offer special discount days. Some even offer free admission on certain days of the month. For performances, ask about free or greatly discounted admission to dress rehearsals.

- *Call your favorite hometown theater* to see if it offers ticket price cuts right before show time; there's a chance a show will sell out, so keep your plans flexible.

- *Check with your community college.* College campuses offer quality entertainment options, including student musical performances, film festivals, art exhibits, theater productions, dance recitals, sporting events and more. Many are free or very inexpensive.

- *Team up for baby-sitting.* A good chunk of any entertainment budget can be chewed up by baby sitter expenses. Join forces with a relative, neighbor or friend and trade off watching each other's kids. For example, you watch their kids one Saturday evening, and they watch yours another weekend. If you spent $40-$50 for one night a month on babysitter costs, you could save at least $500-$600 a year with your co-op, and get out more often.

- *Go with a group.* Buy tickets in bulk to get a discount to many exhibitions and events. Team up with friends, co-workers or relatives to get the lower rate.

- *Spend less on fitness.* Forget the $40-a-month gym membership that'll cost you almost $500 a year. Instead, use your local YMCA, or check out community centers in your area; some may be free or charge a minimal fee. Or better still, walk or run outside, bicycle, and/or invest in some inexpensive free weights.

- *Use online movie rentals.* Spending $5 for a movie at the local video store can add up quickly. If you watch enough movies to make the expense worth it, subscribe to a mail-order service, such as Blockbuster or Netflix. Blockbuster allows you to exchange a viewed mail-in DVD for an in-store DVD and they do the mailing for you; this means your subscription is actually giving you a 2-for-1 deal. It also means you can subscribe to a less costly plan, depending on the terms.

- *Use your library card* to enjoy DVDs and books for free. If you'd normally rent a movie a week and buy a book a month, you can cut costs by $30 a month. Also check out library-sponsored events, such as book readings, film screenings, and lectures.

- *Head outdoors* for a lot of free and healthy entertainment. Go hiking, picnicking, bird watching, fishing, kayaking or camping. You could even host a campout and hot dog roast in your backyard.

Transportation

To estimate the real monthly cost to buy, insure, and operate any given car over five years, double the price tag and divide by 60. This guideline can help you determine if that car you think is affordable actually will be. Overspending on cars or buying the wrong one can cost you a small fortune. Instead of spending money on a new very expensive toy or status symbol, consider the following suggestions:

- *Keep the old car a few more years.* Today's cars are better built and more dependable than ever, which means that unless you've got a real lemon you could keep driving it past 200,000 or even 300,000 miles, assuming you regularly maintain it.

- *If you must buy a car, buy a used one.* This also reduces tax and insurance costs. The average new car loses 12.2% of its value in the first year[11]; on a $20,000 car, that's $2,440, or more than $200 a month. Some cars depreciate even faster. Recent used models that are less than 5 years old can be a real value because you get a nearly new car in fine working order for a fraction of the new-car price. Obviously, the better the gas mileage, the more money you'll save.

  Note: If you must borrow to buy a car, follow the 20/4/10 rule. Make a 20% down payment, don't borrow for more than four years and don't agree to a monthly payment that's more than 10% of your income – 8% if you plan to buy a home in the next few years. A substantial down payment ensures having equity in your car when you drive off the lot (owing more on your car than it's worth can leave you financially vulnerable if it's totaled or stolen). Limiting the loan term and monthly payment will keep you from overspending.

Don't roll debt from a previous car loan to another; this means you'll pay higher interest rates because much of what you owe isn't secured by the car itself. Many auto finance companies make loans knowing that many borrowers will miss payments or default. Lenders count on high interest rates to cover their risks. They don't really care if you can afford the payment or not -- they're gambling on making enough from the loan to profit either way.

- *Avoid leasing.* People who buy cars and drive them for 10 years or more, compared with people who swap out their cars every five years, can save *hundreds of thousands* of dollars on vehicles during their lifetime. The savings compared with those who lease cars are even greater.

- *Examine your car costs.* Your car shouldn't cost you more than a maximum of 20% of your net income, including financing, repairs and gas. Instead of buying a new car, take an auto mechanic course at a community college and get an older reliable model or classic car. The gas mileage hit will never offset the 40 to 60 percent hit you get over five years with a new vehicle. Any older rear-wheel drive is easier to maintain than a front-wheel drive. You won't have all the electronic features with an older car, but you also won't have to pay to get them fixed when they break.

- *Maintain your car regularly,* particularly a lube, oil, and filter service every 3000 miles or every 3 months, whichever comes first, and don't forget the air filter. This will keep your car from needing costly repairs; it will also keep it running and using gas more efficiently.

- *Check your tires.* Properly inflated tires improve gas mileage. Buy a tire gauge, and check your tires *every time* you fill up the tank.

Six areas of maintenance you should never skip:

1. Consistent oil changes
2. Tire rotations (every 6,000 miles) and air pressure checks
3. Replace timing belt
4. Annual brake checkup
5. Replacing the PCV regularly
6. Changing spark plugs and filters

Total cost of maintaining car	Total cost of not maintaining car
$1000+	$8000+

- *Drive less.* With gas price increases, you don't have to cut back on much mileage to save $300-$500 a year. Driving a car that gets 15 miles per gallon just 40 fewer miles per week will save that much in gas alone. Forty miles per week represents only about 6 miles a day, which can easily be eliminated by running numerous errands in one trip and consolidating other multiple trips such as grocery shopping, choosing stores closer to home, driving under 65mph, or carpooling.

- *Re-shop for car insurance.* Using a comparison site such as InsWeb.com can help you determine whether you've got the best deal. Rates vary widely from insurer to insurer. Your savings could equal hundreds of dollars.

- *Reduce your car insurance.* If you drive a car worth less than $2,000, you'll probably pay more to insure it than you would ever collect on a claim. Dropping collision and comprehensive coverage can reduce your premium by one-third.

- *Raise your deductible.* Upping your out-of-pocket outlay from $250 to $1,000 on any car can save you 15% or more on your car insurance. However, make sure you have enough cash in an emergency savings account to cover your deductible so you don't have to rely on costly credit cards in case of an accident.

- *Look for multiple-line insurance.* When shopping around for auto insurance, check first with the company that provides your renters or homeowners insurance. You can get up to 15% off for a multiple-line policy.

- *Shop around for gas.* Gas prices can vary within only a few blocks. So look around or go online to find the best deal in your neighborhood or along your commute route. A 20-cent difference on 60 gallons of gas per month adds up to $12 per month, or $144 per year.

- *Use a gas-rebate credit card* if you use a credit card to pay for your gas. This will help to soften the financial sting by giving you cash back for filling up. For example, a card can give you 5% cash back on gas and auto maintenance charges up to $100 per month. That saves you about $60 per year.

   Note: It's best to use the credit card for gas purchases only and pay off the balance each month so you're not tempted to lose control of your credit (see Credit/Debit).

- *Use public transportation*, if possible, to save on commuting costs. You'll save on the cost of a parking space, gas and auto maintenance. Plus, you can probably get a lower insurance rate for driving less.

- *Car pool.* Sharing the ride and expense with another person can cut your gas costs in half.

If you're already stuck in an unaffordable car situation, you only have a few options:

1. Sell the car if you have some equity in it or can come up with extra cash to pay off the loan; or, if you can

persuade the lender to let you pay off the remaining debt over time.

2. Try to refinance if you bought the car new, made payments for a few years and have a lender who's willing to extend your loan term. For used cars, you need to have some equity in order to be able to refinance.

3. You can let the lender repossess the car. This option should be avoided if at all possible because repossession, voluntary or not, trashes your credit and usually leaves you with substantial debt besides. You'll still owe the difference between your loan balance and whatever the car brings at auction, plus repossession and auction fees.

4. Drive out of the loan. This is usually the best solution for a too-expensive car. Trim other areas of your budget so you can make the payments and keep driving the car until it's paid off; then keep driving it until you've saved up enough to buy another less expensive car, or to at least make a substantial down payment.

The next time you're in the market for a car:

- **Rethink the whole thing.** There must be something else on which you'd rather spend $8,000 a year. With that as motivation, you may be able to find a way to live without a car, or with one less car if yours is a multiple-vehicle family, or to keep the car you have going for a little longer. Think about the options before you commit yourself to another payment.

- **Figure out what you can actually afford.** If you don't have other large expenses, you might get away with higher car costs. If you've got a big mortgage or child-care bills to pay, you might need to spend less. A professor and bankruptcy researcher[12] recommends that all your basic expenses -- shelter, food, insurance, child care, transportation and minimum loan payments -- total no more than 50% of your after-tax income. With this guideline, you're sure to have enough left over for variable expenses like clothing and vacations (30% of after-tax pay) as well as giving you room to pay off debt (20%) and save adequately for retirement.

You might not be anywhere close to this guideline, but it's something to aim for as you get your finances in order. In the meantime, you can simply double your projected car payment and see how well that fits into your budget. Try putting aside the amount of this projected payment each month for three months to see if you can comfortably afford it. If it stretches your budget too thin, look for a cheaper car.

11 Edmunds.com
12 Elizabeth Warren

Children

Two of the biggest expenses for younger children, other than child care, are clothes and toys. We need to be extra careful about children's items – hygiene, safety, and reliability. Keeping this in mind, there are still some ways to reduce these expenses, some of which follow:

- *Swap second-hand clothes and some toys* with other family members or close friends and neighbors if you have no older children with hand-me-downs.

- *Shop consignment shops and yard sales* for new or nearly-new items.

- *Watch flyers and shop online for bargains.*
  Note: When shopping online, always include shipping & handling charges when comparing prices.

- *Don't spend a lot on gifts that children don't want.* Most children are more interested in basic inexpensive items, such as small toy cars; building sets like Lego kits, Lincoln Logs, or erector sets; art supplies; books; and balls. Also, if your child has received numerous toys as birthday or holiday gifts from family and friends, give him/her a few for now, then dole the rest out as interest in the current toy dies. This way your child can have new toys to play with throughout the year instead of for just one day, and his/her interest and creativity will continue to be stimulated.

- *Encourage grandparents and other family members to give one or two simple gifts* (toys or clothes) plus a contribution to the child's college fund, instead of numerous or large gifts. This way, the child will have something to enjoy now and help later toward his/her future.

Travel/Vacation

- *Travel during the off season* to save money and avoid crowds. For instance, if a destination, such as national parks and Canada, has its highest tourist traffic in summer, plan your visit for winter, spring or fall. In summer, head for popular winter destinations, such as ski resorts and Caribbean cruises.

- *Use Kayak.com.* You can waste time and money surfing the Web among Expedia, Orbitz, Cheaptickets, etc. trying to find the cheapest airfare. Instead, go to Kayak.com, which lists fares (plus hotel rates and other travel products) from more than 140 sources and sends you to the site you choose. If your itinerary isn't definite, increase your odds of finding a deal by using the flexible-dates option to search for flights over a range of dates.

- *Bundle your airfare with a hotel or car rental*, especially if you're making last minute travel plans. Airlines discount open seats at the last minute by rolling them into packages, which don't list the fare reduction separately. LastMinute.com is one website that specializes in last minute getaways, which include these bundled packages.

- *Plan a vacation close to home*, within driving distance, to save money. The *Day Trips* series and *Quick Escapes* series[13] offer numerous ideas for vacation itineraries in various cities.

- *Check out a tour guide book for your city* from your local library, and tour your own hometown -- something many of us neglect to think of doing.

- *Negotiate hotel room rates.* Independent and regional chain hotels that lack the marketing power of national chains may be more willing to bargain to fill an unexpected vacancy for free or at a discounted rate. Ask the front desk for an extra night's stay for free or at a discounted rate, even if the hotel isn't currently advertising one. Tell them you already have a reservation at another hotel at a cheaper rate, but you'd rather stay with them if they give you an extra night for free.

- *Stay at a campsite,* if it suits you. This can save you a whole lot of money. Recreation.gov handles reservations for the U.S. Forest Service, National Park Service and others. There are many campsites for about $20 a night at various locations, including mountain sites and beachfronts.

- *Try hostelling* (similar to dorm rooms), for only about $20-$30 a night. You can make reservations online through Hostels.com. Many hostels also offer private rooms for couples or families for a little more money.

- *Book your travel through blind-booking sites* such as Hotwire.com and Priceline.com for substantial savings. For example, on rental cars, airfare, or hotels you specify the dates and locations, but you don't find out which company is offering you your nonrefundable rate until after you buy.

- *Try a small inn or a bed and breakfast instead of a hotel.* These operations are often more flexible about discounting to fill vacancies. One way to find B&B bargains is to sign up for free weekly e-mails from Bedandbreakfast.com. Every Wednesday, they send you a list of places offering deals of 20% or more off regular rates for the upcoming weekend in the city, state or region you prefer to visit.

- *Consider a vacation condo or house rental,* which generally offer more room and amenities for the same price as hotel rooms. Plus, their kitchens can spare you from having to dine out for every meal. Vacation with family or friends, and share the costs for even greater savings and more fun.

- *Look for cruise cancellations.* When people who booked a cruise early cancel at the last minute, staterooms become available at bargain prices. Check with a cruise travel agent, or search SkyAuction.com or Moments-Notice.com.

- *Sign up for an airline's frequent flier program.* Enrollment is free, and you can sign up with every airline you fly with. Then, cash in your earned miles for free flights, hotel stays, merchandise and other perks.

- *Bid for travel at Priceline.com* to save money on airfare, car rentals, and especially hotels (sometimes $100 or less). Recent bidders post their bid successes on Biddingfortravel.com; you can refer to that before bidding at Priceline to help you submit the lowest winning bid.

13 Globe Pequot Press

Clothing

- *Learn how to sew and mend* things such as buttons, socks, and even jewelry, extending their life -- "Wear it out, or do without."
- *Don't buy clothes or accessories if you don't really need them.* If you shop just for fun or out of boredom, you may need to avoid all clothing stores for a while to break the habit. Not buying clothes for a few months can also give you a better idea of what you really wear and need.
- *Shop at thrift and consignment shops.* You'll be surprised at how many items were never even worn and still have the tags on! Buy used clothing, accessories and jewelry whenever possible.
- *Swap clothes and accessories with family and friends,* and if they're planning to get rid of some clothes that are still in good condition, don't be too proud to ask if you can have them.
- *Attend a garage sale instead of going to the mall* – "One man's trash is another man's treasure"
- *Buy solid colors and timeless prints that won't go out of style.* Don't buy based on what's "in style", buy what fits you best and looks best on you.
- *Buy no-wrinkle clothes.* Many clothes now are of wrinkle free material. Try not to buy anything that requires ironing, and you'll be more likely to wear it frequently and get the most use out of it.
- *Make a list.* As with grocery shopping, a list can help you resist impulse purchases and make sure you get what you truly need and are shopping for.
- *Get help if you can't not shop.* Sometimes shopping, especially for clothing which may more easily be justified as being necessary, is a symptom of a more troubling disorder. Read Appendix A, "Are you a compulsive shopper?", for more details.

Personal Care & Hygiene

- *Take a "Navy" shower.* Get in, soap up, rinse off and get out. Also, get a low-flow showerhead to conserve water and money.

- *Reuse bath towels.* You're clean when you get out of the shower, so the towel is only soaking up water. Hang towels after each use to thoroughly dry, and only add them to the laundry after every three or four uses.

- *Don't run water when shaving or brushing teeth.* When shaving, use the sink stopper to pool a little water in the sink for rinsing your razor.

- *Skip baths,* which require a lot of water and drive up your water bill. They also drain your supply of hot water, forcing your hot water heater to replenish and further increasing your utility costs.

- *Don't throw out bar soap* until it's so small it starts breaking into little pieces.

- *Eliminate waste and expense by using only as much liquid soap or shampoo as is necessary.* When they're down to the last few drops, add a little water to the container to get one or two more uses.

- *Roll up the bottom of the toothpaste tube* to squeeze as much out as possible before throwing it away.

- *Buy store brand or no-name hygiene products* for substantial savings. Also buy in larger quantities for lower per-ounce costs – remember to do the math first.

Employment

- *Update your W-4.* If you received a tax refund this year, the fastest way to give yourself a raise is to reduce the amount of taxes withheld from your paycheck by increasing the number of exemptions on your W-4. Getting a tax refund only means you've allowed the government the use of your money, which could have been earning savings interest. At the IRS website, calculate the number of exemptions required to break even, which should be your goal.

- *Learn new skills and stay employed.* During tough economies, companies assess the contributions each employee makes. If you sense downsizing and your job may be at risk, increase your skills to enhance your value at work and to decrease your chances of being let go. You may also be able to use these new skills to earn some extra income by freelancing or consulting on the side, or to secure a higher paying position with your current company or elsewhere. If losing your job is inevitable and you don't have anything else immediately lined up, don't resign. Recession is extremely difficult if you're unemployed, so stay to continue getting a paycheck, and you might be able to negotiate some favorable severance terms before having to go back to the marketplace.

Pets

Pets can be very expensive. While the value of animal companionship can't be denied, if you're considering a pet, keep the cost of upkeep in mind. The following averages include food, medical care and various accessories:

First year costs of common pets			
Small bird	$195	Small dog	$810
Fish	$235	Rabbit	$911
Guinea pig	$645	Medium dog	$1,190
Cat	$715	Large dog	$1,580

Source: ASPCA

If your animal gets sick or hurt, your costs could skyrocket. You may want to consider pet health insurance; the oldest pet insurer is Veterinary Pet Insurance.

Health & Fitness

- *Use your prescription mail-in program.* Many employers now offer a 3-month mail order prescription plan whereby you can get a 90-day supply of your prescription drug at a great discount. For example, using your health insurance coverage to fill a prescription at the pharmacy may cost you $25 for a 30-day supply; the same prescription mailed in may only cost you $50 for a 90-day supply – a further savings of $25 and fewer trips to the pharmacy.

- *Sign up for medical flexible spending account* (FSA) at work if it is offered. Account for the amount of your family's health care plan deductibles and co-pays plus any over-the-counter medical supplies you must purchase during the year. Estimate carefully, since unused portions of FSAs are not refundable. As an added bonus, FSA contributions are pre-tax, which lowers your taxable income for the year.

- *Quit smoking.* Besides being an incredibly unhealthy habit, smoking is also incredibly expensive. If you can't find any other motivation to quit, use finances.

- *Evaluate fitness equipment expenditures.* A lot of money is spent on exercise equipment that goes unused. No workout system can deliver commitment, regardless of good intentions. Unless you're already engaged in a regular fitness routine, think twice about investing in home equipment.

- *Go outdoors.* Walking, running, biking and swimming are comparatively low-cost ways to stay healthy. Try those first.

- *Don't renew the gym membership.* Take the money you would have spent at the gym and try to build one at home with inexpensive (free weights, fitness ball, tubes) and used equipment (stationary bike, treadmill, elliptical).

Look in your local community paper; shop Play It Again Sports store; visit yard sales; and shop online at Craigslist, E-Bay, Amazon.com, or Overstock.com.

Appendix A
Are you a compulsive shopper?[14]

Answer "often," "sometimes," "rarely" or "never."

- Do you buy things you want, whether or not you can afford them at the moment?
- Do you have trouble saving money? If you have a little extra available to save or invest, do you tend to think of something you'd rather spend it on?
- Do you buy things to cheer yourself up or to reward yourself?
- Does more than a third of your income, not including rent or mortgage payments, go to pay bills?
- Do you juggle bill paying because you always seem to be living on the edge financially?
- Do you tend to keep buying more of your favorite things even if you don't have a specific need for them?
- If you have to deny yourself or put off buying something you really want, do you feel intensely deprived, angry or upset?

If you answered "often" or "sometimes" to four or more questions, you're probably a compulsive spender, especially if you answered "often" or "sometimes" to the last question. It is far more complex than financial disorganization or irresponsibility; compulsive spending is an addiction that can consume a person's life.

Some other questions that might help you decide if you're a compulsive shopper come from the compulsive buying scale[15], which includes some predictors of compulsive shoppers:

- Others may be "horrified" by your spending habits.

- You write checks when you know you don't have enough money in the bank to cover them.
- You go shopping to feel better.
- You feel bad if you don't go shopping.
- You feel like you have to spend money if you have any left over at the end of the month.

More common among women than men, compulsive shopping often accompanies other mental-health problems, including depression, alcoholism and eating disorders. Sufferers tend to target certain items. For women, it's usually clothes or shoes; for men, it's often electronics or books. Sufferers tend not to use the things they buy, storing them, returning them, or giving them away.

The essence of the problem, like any addiction, stems from low self-esteem, insecurity and inadequacy; or, from a person not knowing how to get what they need emotionally any other way.

Steps to recovery

As with any addiction, the first step is admitting there is a problem and wanting help. Programs such as Debtors Anonymous and/or credit counseling are beneficial, along with therapy sessions. Unlike alcoholics who can abstain from drinking and drug addicts who can swear off drugs, recovery for a compulsive shopper is a challenge because people have to buy things.

Some initial steps to recovery are:
- Give up credit cards; get rid of all plastic.
- Never buy anything spontaneously; go shopping with a list, and don't buy anything that isn't on the list. If you see something you want, wait 24 hours before you buy it.

- Stay away from garage sales, home shopping channels on TV, and online shopping sites.
- Identify specific times of the day or week, such as payday at a job you don't like, when you could be tempted to shop; then, make a list of other behaviors you can substitute for shopping, such as exercising, taking a bath, walking, doing something creative, calling a friend, volunteering or making a "community or spiritual connection."

14 Quiz developed by Olivia Mellan
15 Co-developed by Ron Faber

Appendix B

90 Low Cost or No Cost Activities to Entertain Your Kids All Summer Long
by: Debbie Dragon

Outdoor Activities

1. **Make sailboats and race them.** Put water in a plastic kid's pool and race your handmade sailboats. Use only the natural wind power to make them go and see who makes it to the finish line first!

2. **Jump rope**. This is fun for one child or a group of children. Learn a few songs and games to play for group jump roping, and try to see how many jumps each person can make before making a mistake.

3. **Puddle jumping**. Nothing is more fun than getting to play outside when it's raining. Summer rainstorms don't always mean you have to head inside- put on bathing suits and rain boots and stomp in the puddles!

4. **Have your own drive-in movie.** On a clear, dry night, bring the television set outdoors and let the kids watch a movie on blankets under the stars. For added fun, invite the neighborhood kids to drive-in on their bicycles to enjoy the movie, too. Don't forget the popcorn!

5. **Plant a container garden.** Many vegetables and herbs can be grown indoors or out inside containers. Let your children pick some varieties to grow and tend to them throughout the summer. It may even convince them to eat a vegetable if they know they grew it!

6. **Target squirting.** Set plastic cups on the top of a fence, deck railing, or balanced on kids heads and let other children squirt them off with water guns or plastic water bottles. You can create

points by writing on the plastic cups and keep score or just see who's the fastest to knock over the cups.

7. **Car wash.** Arm your kids with the hose, a bucket, soap and some sponges and set them to work washing the family car (and each other). You could let them hang a sign around town advertising their car wash service, as well.

8. **Dirt restaurant.** Kids love to play restaurant, and who doesn't love to play in the dirt? Send the kids outside with plastic cups and plastic spoons, a few dollar store dishes and see what kind of gourmet meals they come up with. They can make salads from leaves and flower petals, mud pies, and tree bark chicken. The kids can take turns making meals, being waiters and restaurant patrons.

9. **Water balloons.** An always fun, but often forgotten activity, water balloons are easy to make and cheap! Fill some balloons with water and play water balloon toss- start kids standing close together and each time the balloon is caught without breaking everyone takes a step back!

10. **Go for a hike, walk or bike ride.** Most towns have parks and areas that are perfect for this, but even if you have to make it a full day trip and travel a bit, this is a great activity to beat summer time boredom. Pack a picnic lunch and plenty of fluids and enjoy some exercise.

11. **Oversized painting.** Tape several large sheets of paper together on the backside, and flip them over on the lawn. Fill a few containers with different colors of finger paints, and give the kids a box of strange items to make their painting with. Try: spaghetti strainer, a balloon, a mop head, sponges, rain boots and any other objects you see lying around!

12. **Bubbles.** Just about every kid enjoys bubbles! Create your own bubble solution with dishwashing liquid, water, and a teaspoon of sugar. Pour into a shallow container with a wide open mouth and then use odd objects to create your bubbles. String, rubber

bands, the spaghetti strainer, straws, slotted spoons and anything else you can think of make some fun bubbles!

13. **Bubble art.** When the kids tired of making bubbles, add a few drops of food coloring to the bubble solution and have them blow bubbles that pop onto white paper. The result will be an artistic masterpiece made from the rainbow colored bubbles!

14. **Sand art.** Use food coloring to color sand in Ziploc bags. Pour the sand on paper plates to dry before using. Once dry, glue to paper to make cards and art; or fill plastic containers with your sand art creations.

15. **Make a sandbox.** For whatever reason, kids like playing in the dirt! You can make an inexpensive sandbox by filling a kid size plastic pool with clean dirt you dig up from your yard, or from sand you purchase from the store. Fill with plastic trucks and plastic cups and let the kids go to town.

16. **Organize sports days.** If you live in an area where there are many children, you may be able to organize a day every week to play sports. Set up a baseball team, soccer team or other sports team and get the kids active. Just be sure to have enough water near by- especially if it's hot!

17. **Sidewalk Chalk.** Drawing on the ground is always fun. You can let the kids make pictures and drawings, or use it to make hopscotch and other games to play on the sidewalk.

18. **Create race car track.** If you have miniature cars (hot wheels and others), it can be tons of fun to create elaborate race tracks in the dirt, complete with jumps, water pits and crash areas.

19. **Water games.** You can let the kids run through the sprinklers, wade in a kiddie pool, spray each other with the hose, or play with a bucket full of water and plastic cups. They'll be creative with it; or they'll just get each other wet but either way they'll have fun doing it.

20. **Organize a bike parade.** Gather as many neighborhood kids as you can, and have everyone decorate their bikes like parade floats. Parade around the driveways or through a bike path.

21. **Collect cans and bottles.** Take your kids through the town and collect as many bottles and cans as you can. Return them to the store and give the kids the money to buy themselves a treat. It will take up an afternoon, give the kids exercise, and help the environment all at the same time.

22. **Scavenger Hunt.** Create a list of 20 or more things that can be found naturally outside in your area, things like pinecones, specific flowers, nuts, etc. Send the kids on a scavenger hunt to try and collect one of each item on the list. This can be done as a group effort, or each child can compete with the other to see who can find the most objects, the fastest.

23. **Set up an obstacle course**. Turn your backyard into an amazing obstacle course! Let the kids create a course from toys, bikes, and other things found in your backyard. Just keep an eye on them so they aren't doing anything that would be unsafe!

24. **Go to yard sales**. Give each child a few dollars and allow them to make purchases at a few yard sales. The new-to-them items are always more fun than the items they already own (at least for a couple hours!) You could do the same thing at the dollar store.

25. **Go fishing**. Borrow fishing poles if you don't have any and spend the day fishing in a river, lake or pond.

26. **Visit every playground**. Determine how many playgrounds are within a 25 mile radius of your home, and pick one day a week as playground day. Try to get a few other families to join you; and visit one park each week.

27. **Build a rock garden.** For some reason, kids really enjoy rocks. Let them collect various rocks and arrange them in a nice garden. For added fun, they could paint the rocks.

28. **Visit a local farm.** You can probably pick fresh berries at the start of summer, and apples towards the end of summer. Some farms have activities like hay rides, horseback riding and a petting zoo.

29. **Make a slip n' slide**. Use an old tarp as a slip n' slide, or buy one. The kids will enjoy this activity for a few hours on a hot summer day.

30. **Go to drive-in movie**. While you don't want to spend all day every day in front of the TV or movie theatre; there is no harm in catching a movie or two. Drive-ins are less expensive and you can enjoy the outdoors while you watch the movie.

31. **Stargaze**. Take a blanket out after it gets dark, a flashlight and an astronomy guide. See if you can find all the constellations.

32. **Have a campout.** You don't have to actually go anywhere to go "camping". Pitch a tent in the backyard, build a fire (if local laws allow), toast marshmallows and enjoy camping in the backyard.

Indoor Activities

33. **Crafts.** You can purchase a bunch of craft supplies and let your children's imaginations lead them to the creation of masterpieces. The local dollar store often has a good selection of craft supplies, and if not- Wal-Mart or the craft store have a good variety that won't hurt your wallet too much. Alternatively, you can probably dig up enough craft-stuff from around your house for a few hours of creating: buttons, glue, string, macaroni noodles- if it can be glued, it can work!

34. **Indoor camping.** Throw a sheet over your kitchen table and camp out underneath. You can sing campfire songs, make s'mores in the microwave, and pretend to go fishing. If you have a small pop-tent, these can be set up indoors temporarily, too and provide hours of entertainment.

35. **Make a puzzle.** Draw a picture or cut one from a magazine. Cut it into puzzle shapes and then put it back together.

36. **Play volleyball**. Yes, you can play this version of volleyball inside. You just need a blow up beach ball and your couch. Pull the couch into the middle of the room so you can stand on either side of it, and use it as your volleyball net. (You could also drape a sheet over a couple of chairs to create your net)

37. **Papier-mâché stuff**. Mix water and flour in a bowl to create a paste. Cut up strips of newspapers and make papier-mâché objects. You can make piñatas, decorative items or animal creations. Just remember it takes several days for it to dry before you can paint and decorate it (or before you can break it open if you've made a piñata!)

38. **Make puppets**. Use socks and craft supplies from around the house to create puppets and put on a puppet show.

39. **5-Minute Make-Your-Own- Ice Cream**. In a quart Ziploc bag, put in a cup of milk, a teaspoon of vanilla and sugar. In a gallon Ziploc bag, put in a 1/3 of a cup of salt and fill the bag ¾ of the way full with ice cubes. Place the smaller bag inside the larger bag, and shake for 5 minutes. Open and serve!

40. **Become a dancing fool.** If you feel like you've been cooped up inside for too long due to bad weather or other reasons, put on some upbeat music and dance until you're too tired to dance anymore! The sillier you are, the better!

41. **Create the beach.** If the beach is too far away or the weather causes you to stay inside, turn your bathtub into the ocean! Younger kids will get a kick out of this activity. Fill your tub with some cool water, play some beach tunes and give the kids the sand toys to play with in the tub in their bathing suits. Blow up a beach ball for some extra fun.

42. **Café Kids**. Let the kids create restaurant menus of items you have in your kitchen and then take turns taking lunch orders from each other (or you). Let everyone be the kitchen staff to

prepare the lunches, and then switch to become the customers who get to eat the delicious meals they've ordered!

43. **Draw mazes**. On paper, create mazes and let your kids try to get to the end point. If you have a hamster or guinea pig, create a maze out of cardboard and see if it can find the end of the maze.

44. **Start an activity co-op**. If you are good at arts and crafts, your friend is good at yoga, someone else knows gymnastics or plays an instrument, etc- you could all get together and start an activity co-op. Once a week, each parent could host an activity at their home for everyone's kids throughout the summer. It's a low cost way to keep the kids involved in various activities.

45. **Indoor picnic.** Spread a blanket out on the living room floor and have an indoor picnic. No bugs!

46. **Scrapbook**. If you have a digital camera, consider letting the children take photos throughout the summer and get the best ones printed. Alternatively, you could buy a few disposable cameras for them to use. Using your craft supplies, create mini scrapbooks of what the kids did over their summer vacation.

47. **Put on a talent show**. Let the kids practice their talents, create tickets and flyers to give to the neighbors, and invite everyone to watch their performance. Let the neighborhood kids participate in the talent show, too! You can hold it inside or out; and give every participant a certificate and a round of applause.

48. **Make a dream book**. Using magazines, let the children cut out photographs and draw pictures of things they'd like to have someday, places they'd like to go, careers they'd like to have one day and glue them into a dream book.

49. **Start making holiday gifts for family.** Use all the free time you have in the summer to start on your holiday gift list. The kids can make photo frames, mini scrapbooks, and craft items to give as gifts throughout the year.

50. **Tie Dye**. You can buy a kit or just get the colors from the craft store (or department store). You'll need socks or tee shirts or whatever else you want to tie dye, and rubber bands, as well as rubber gloves to protect your skin from the dye. Alternatively, you could try using berries to create your own dyes.

51. **Marble games**. Buy a big bag of marbles (really inexpensive!) and make up games to play with them. You can also search online for marble games and learn a few new ones.

52. **Room rearranging.** Let the children draw a new layout of their bedroom(s) on paper, and then help them move everything around into their new configuration.

53. **Go roller skating**. If you have a roller skating rink in your town or near by, watch for special discounts. Many roller rinks offer $2 skating days, which would mean a very inexpensive outing that everyone can enjoy.

54. **Organize a block party.** Get everyone on your street or block together for a block party. Have face painting, activities, music and dancing, karaoke, and food (pot luck works great!).

55. **Go swimming**. If you aren't lucky enough to have your own pool, you can visit the park pool on a day pass, visit a friend or family member with a pool, or go to the lake for a day of swimming. Beat the heat and get some exercise at the same time.

56. **Set up a net**. Put up a badminton or volleyball net, or create one from clothes line and a sheet. Use a blow up beach ball to play volleyball or get a badminton set from a yard sale and play.

57. **Soccer bowling.** Set up 10 empty soda cans or plastic bottles in a triangle or circle on a fairly level section in your yard or driveway. Give each child three tries to knock down as many "pins" as possible by kicking an inflated ball at them from at least 20 feet away. Keep score like bowling.

58. **Make fruit Popsicles**. Make your own fruit juice Popsicles with juice in paper cups and Popsicle sticks in them. Pop in the freezer until frozen and serve.

59. **Host a sleepover**. Let your children invite a few friends over for a sleepover. It's a fun way to break up the routine. The kids can play board games, watch a movie, make and eat fun snacks and enjoy some social time.

60. **Act out your favorite book or movie**. Get the family together and/or invite some friends over to help re-enact a fairy tale or favorite scene from a book.

61. **Learn a new language**. Use the internet or rent videos and/ or audio instructions to learn a new language.

Educational Activities Your Kids Will Actually Enjoy Doing

62. **Write and Illustrate a book**. With construction paper and some crayons, your children can become authors and illustrators. If old enough, let them write their own stories and illustrate them (either by drawing pictures or cutting photos out of old magazines); for younger children, you can write down their story as they dictate it to you.

63. **Visit the museum**. (or the planetarium, the botanical gardens, etc) Most locations have a museum or other low-admission attraction that would make a nice day-trip. Not only is it something you don't do every day, but it's fun and educational, too.

64. **Volunteering**. The local retirement home and hospital often like when kids come in to help serve lunch, or read to the patients. Alternatively, your children could volunteer at the animal shelter- they always need help making sure the dogs get out for some exercise!

65. **Make your own board games.** Playing board games is fun for all ages, but can get a little boring when you play the same

games, over and over. Spend some time creating your own board game with cardboard, crayons and other objects- then play it! The real fun is the creation of the game itself, but you can play and save the game for future playtime as well.

66. **Lemonade stand.** Turn your children into mini-entrepreneurs! Teach them how to figure out their profits by subtracting the cost of their materials and supplies and how many cups of lemonade they sell.

67. **Yard sale.** Help the kids organize a yard sale. They can price their unused toys and clothing and other items that it's time to get rid of, set up the tables outside with the items to sell, and handle the "customers". Anything that doesn't sell can be placed on eBay or another online auction site; and the kids could use the money to buy themselves a new summertime activity.

68. **Make a Movie/Play.** If you have a video camera, let the kids write, direct, act, and record their own movies. If you don't have one and can't borrow one, you can do the same thing but have a live performance- like a play.

69. **Treasure Hunt.** Hide a small treasure (a bag of candy, new game, etc) some where in the house. Then use post-its to write clues. Each clue will lead to another clue, until finally the last one will lead the children to the "treasure".

70. **Simulate Stocks**. For older children, use the newspaper or internet to research stocks and pretend to buy shares. Monitor the stocks throughout the summer and see whether you make or lose money.

71. **Computer time.** Find a few educational websites and let your children use them on a day when they can't go outside to play or are looking for something to do. Most kids love computers and there are thousands of websites designed to educate and entertain at the same time. http://www.funbrain.com/ is a good source. (You could even enroll older kids into a summer online course if

you wanted- they have courses in music, writing, as well as all the typical academics.)

72. **Preserve the kids' school work**. Many parents like to keep some of the kids school work each year. Let the kids pick out a few favorites from each year they've been in school and create a book out of them. You can slide worksheets and artwork into page protectors to store in a binder; scan the documents into your computer to create a digital file, or glue a few pages onto construction paper and bind together into a booklet.

73. **Make music together.** Write song lyrics and come up with a melody. Record on your computer, mp3 player or tape recorder as a special keepsake.

74. **Play store**. Either purchase a toy cash register from the store, or set up a calculator at the check out station. Make or buy play money, and spend an afternoon buying items and making change. You could even make a pretend check register and write checks, depending how old your children are.

75. **Create a chore chart**. On a dry erase board or piece of cardboard, design a chore chart with the kids and give stickers or stars whenever their chores are accomplished. Set small goals and rewards for each week. It will give the kids responsibilities and something to look forward to during the summer weeks.

76. **Teach children to cook.** Use easy recipes, but take advantage of all the learning opportunities involved with cooking: creating the shopping list, sticking to a budget, using measuring cups and spoons, nutrition, and actually making the meal.

77. **Learn origami.** Get a book that teaches origami, or look up origami instructions online. Learn how to make several origami shapes and animals.

78. **Cartoon flipbooks.** Show your children how to staple paper together or use a notebook and draw images that are slightly different from one page to the next so that when they flip through the pages, they appear to be moving.

79. **Start a book club**. Ideally, you could get a few kids around the same age to all read the same book and get together to chat about it; but if there isn't enough participation, even a parent and child could read the same book and have a discussion about it.

80. **Color carnations.** Buy white carnations from a florist or grocery store, and place them in cups with food coloring mixed with water. After awhile, the flowers will take on the colors of the water they're in.

81. **Play school.** Take turns being the teacher and the students, and make worksheets and activities for the students to complete.

82. **Zoos.** Find a near by zoo and spend a day there. The admission may be a bit on the steep side, but you can often pack snacks and lunches to prevent having to pay for anything other than the entry price and the educational and fun opportunities at the zoo are endless!

83. **Geocaching.** This is a free activity for older kids and teenagers-or the entire family can participate. Visit this website: http://www.geocaching.com/ and enjoy a high-tech treasure hunt!

84. **Keep a Journal.** Have your children write daily in a journal. They can write about what they did that day, or what they hope to do the next day.

85. **Be a tourist**. Pretend to be a tourist in your own town and near by locations. Use maps to discover landmarks, attractions and parks that you've never gone to, and plan family trips to visit each.

86. **Savings Account.** Help your child learn responsible money skills by taking them to the local bank to open a savings account. Help them discover ways of earning money throughout the summer and teach them about saving and interest.

87. **Go to the library.** Visit the library once a week and allow children to check out books to read. Check into activities –

most libraries hold children's' activities or crafts throughout the summer.

88. **Toss a ball.** Have everyone sit in a circle. Every time they have the ball, they say a name of a state (or animal, or food, etc) that starts with the next letter of the alphabet as they throw the ball to someone else.

89. **Google earth**. Use Google earth and maps to explore new territory.

90. **Get a Rubik's Cube.** Vow to complete it before the end of summer. You may have to spend time on it every day, and it can be an individual activity or one the entire family takes part in.

Appendix C

Building Wealth
by William Artzberger, CFA

To accumulate wealth over time, you need to do three things:

1. **You need to make it**. This means that before you can begin to save or invest, you need to have a long-term source of income that's sufficient enough to have some left over after you've covered your necessities. You may also consider diversifying your income -- look for ways to increase your income outside of your full time job. Consider building a hobby into a small business. Spend some time working <u>online surveys</u> (many of these companies are scams, but <u>CashCrate</u> is an example of one that's not. Add some freelance work in the same line of work you do full time.

2. **You need to save it.** Once you have an income that's enough to cover your basics, you need to develop a proactive savings plan. *See Saving.*

3. **You need to invest it.** Once you've set aside a monthly savings goal, you need to invest it prudently.

Getting rich is simpler than you think
By Harry Domash

Here is the single most important thing you will ever hear about investing: Getting rich is simple. Not easy, but simple. And here is the second most important thing you will ever hear about investing: You have no excuse not to do it. Only three ingredients are needed: income, discipline and time. Chances are you already have two of them, income and time. All you need to do is add the third, discipline. And armed with the following knowledge, that key third ingredient may be a lot easier to find.

Here's how it works: Say you start with nothing, invest $500 (of your income) a month (a healthy discipline), and let your money ride (over time) in diversified investments. Long term, the stock market returns at least 10% annually. Assuming a 10% return, you'd have $102,000 after 10 years, $380,000 after 20 years, and $1.1 million in 30 years.

Here's a similar scenario: If you start with a nut of $50,000 and add only $250 per month, you'd have $180,000, $516.000 and $1.4 million after 10, 20, and 30 years, respectively. All this happens through the power of regular investing and a simple-but-powerful concept called compounding.

Compounding

What is compounding?

Compounding is the reinvestment of the interest you receive from the money you set aside. For example, if you invest $1,000 and earn 10% interest on your principal at the end of each year, you'll get $100 interest at the end of the first year. If you reinvest that interest, the second year you would start with $1,100, and thus would earn $110 interest. If you stay with it, you'd more than double your money every eight years.

The real magic of investing comes when you combine the surprising power of compounding with continuous and regular investments -- in other words, discipline. The best way to make these continuous investments happen is by setting up an account with a broker or mutual fund that automatically deducts a fixed amount from your bank account every month. "Automatic" is the operative word here. If you don't set it up that way, it won't happen. Instead, you'll end up pouring money in when the market is soaring and skipping payments when it's heading down. Eventually you'll get discouraged and give up.

Dollar-cost averaging

The process of continuously investing a fixed dollar amount is called dollar-cost. Through dollar-cost averaging, you'll end up buying more shares when a stock or fund is down, and fewer when it's up. For instance, say you're investing $500 monthly in a stock trading initially at $50 per share; so the first time, you buy 10 shares. If the next month the stock moves up to $62.50 your regular purchase will net you only eight shares. However, if the stock drops to $41.67, you'll get 12 shares (not including any transaction fees).

It's easy to set up regular-investment mechanisms, thus harnessing the power of dollar-cost averaging. Mutual funds are the traditional way. But there are other outlets, as well, that allow you to apply the strategy with individual stocks or exchange-traded funds, which are baskets of stocks that identically track standard market indexes, such as the Dow Jones Industrial Average ($INDU).

Risk

Investing in the stock market has risk. There's always the chance the market will go nowhere for the next 20 or 30 years and you'll end up no better than where you started. But there's risk in everything, even CDs.

With CDs, your original investment isn't in danger. Most CDs are insured, and the federal government will step in and make you whole, even if your bank goes belly up. But a problem crops up when something more sinister surfaces: inflation. Your real return is the interest you receive less the inflation rate. If your CD is paying 3% and the inflation rate is 2%, you're only making 1% in real terms. If inflation rises to 5%, your CD will probably be paying around 4%. In inflation-adjusted terms, you've lost 1%. But it can get worse. Inflation hit 14% in the early 1980s. In such times, CDs and similar fixed-income investments don't even come close to the inflation rate, meaning you're losing serious money, in real terms.

By contrast, assets such as real estate and stocks tend to move with prices, and, over time, the stock market has outpaced inflation. For instance, in the 20-year period ending Dec. 31, 2001, the cumulative return of the market, as measured by the S&P 500 Index ($INX), was 1,606%, compared to 88% cumulative inflation over the same period.

Yes, there's risk in investing in the market, but the odds are that continuous, regular investing combined with the power of compounding will make you rich.

The Odds

If you count yourself a member of the "I want it now" generation, the idea of waiting 20 or 30 years to get rich probably sounds like a dumb idea. Sure, there are faster ways to get rich. You could win the lottery, or pick the next **Intel** (INTC, news, msgs) or **Wal-Mart Stores** (WMT, news, msgs). But don't quit your day job just yet. Your chances of winning big in the lottery run around 15 million to 1, at best.

Meantime, naturally, you would be sitting pretty if you had had the foresight to plunk significant cash into Intel or Wal-Mart 20 years ago. But consider this: You would have lost money if you'd picked **Advanced Micro Devices** (AMD, news, msgs) instead of Intel, and you'd be broke if you'd picked **Kmart** (SHLD, news, msgs) (which ended up merging with Sears Roebuck) instead of Wal-Mart. In both instances, your retirement plans would be history.

Here's the bottom line: The fate of your retirement, your comfort in older age, probably lies in your commitment to the concepts laid out in the paragraphs above. For the vast majority of us, wealth creation is a slow and steady -- and powerful -- process. The tortoise almost always beats the hare. It's not easy. But it's very, very simple.

Resources

William Artzberger, CFA

Bankrate.com
  Contributors:
    Margarette Burnette
    Pat Curry
    Sheyna Steiner

Debbie Dragon

MSN Money
  Contributors:
    Karen Datko
    Harry Domash
    MP Dunleavey
    Donna Freedman
    The Simple Dollar
    Liz Pulliam Weston

PNC Bank

U.S. News & World Report

U.S. PIRG